47 WAYS TO RAISE PRICES — WITHOUT LOSING CUSTOMERS

MARLENE JENSEN

JGF PRESS

DISCLAIMER

Published December 1, 2020 by
JGF Press, Lock Haven PA
© 2020 Marlene Jensen
eBook-Amazon ISBN: 978-1-7361953-0-7
ePub ISBN: 978-1-7361953-1-4
Print ISBN: 978-1-7355815-6-9
Web Sites & E-Mail:
Jensen at PricingPsychology dot com
http://PricingPsychologyInstitute.com
http://PricingPsychology.com

INTRODUCTION

Welcome to the most practical book you'll ever find on pricing. It is designed for easy understanding and quick implementation of these tactics into your own business.

The goal: for you to start earning higher profits as quickly as possible.

It is organized as an "idea book" for your success. It's divided into 9 sections—depending upon how the price-raising tips in each section can be accomplished:

1. Customer changes
2. Price-only changes
3. Product changes
4. Positioning changes
5. Packaging changes
6. Distribution changes
7. Promotion-only changes
8. Negotiating/salesperson changes
9. Price-change opportunities provided by your competitors

How to use this book

If you are not limited as to the types of changes you can consider, then you may wish to read through the book to grab any "low-hanging fruit"—ideas you know would work and you can implement quickly.

After that, you may wish to reread each of the 46 ideas—one a day. Examine each idea for a day, seeing if there isn't some way to make this work for your industry and your products or services.

If you are unable to make product changes, you can skip that section until later. After a string of successes, management may be more willing to consider broader changes.

Warning about price changes

Each tactic you will read in this book has worked for some companies and some industries. That does not automatically mean it will work for yours.

The marketers among you will know that there are two steps to great marketing decisions:

1. Get a great idea
2. Test it—to make sure it will work for your customers

This book will give you 47 great ideas. Only testing will uncover which of them will work for your customers, your industry, and your circumstances.

PART I

TARGET CUSTOMER CHANGES THAT LET
YOU RAISE PRICES

Sometimes the most profitable thing you can do is change your target customers.

Or . . . maybe you have some customers you should drop!

"Firing" some of your customers can give you the same boost to your bottom line as raising prices.

1

Drop unprofitable customers

One of the great benefits marketers derived from Peppers & Rogers and their introduction of the idea of 1-to-1 marketing is the idea of different treatment for unprofitable customers.

In 1-to-1 marketing, you divide your customers into at least three, preferably four groups. Your "A" customers are those most profitable to your company, who deserve more attention, quicker response times, and more careful handling than the others.

On the other side of the customer-value scale, you should drop any customers who are losing you money.

HOWEVER . . . make sure that the customers you peg as losing you money are not profitable in some other manner (e.g., recommending you to other, more profitable, customers).

Identify and stop promoting to unprofitable customers

How can a customer lose you money? You might be spending $8 a year per customer, sending catalogs. Some of your customers might spend with you, on average, $40 a year, of which $5 is gross profit—before the cost of mailing the catalogs. By stopping any marketing to this customer, you will increase your annual net profits by $3. Multiply that by many more "bad" customers, and you could save yourself a bundle.

Quantifying the effect of "problem" clients

Or . . . you might have six consulting clients, one of whom demands a huge amount of hand-holding. You need to know exactly how much time you are spending on each customer, including those many little 5 minute bits of time answering phone questions. Those small minutes can really add up for some clients.

Not quantifying the effect of time-intensive clients is one of the biggest pricing mistakes made by people launching small service businesses, such as consulting, freelance writing, accounting, etc. When you start, you take any client you can get and are grateful. Then one day, you may find yourself very busy. Not necessarily all the time, but sometimes you are fully booked.

Further, you find most of your work is becoming a flat fee for the work, instead of a billing based on the time you spend. And, unless you have a financial background, you probably don't keep careful track of ALL the time you spend on each project.

Give yourself a fat price increase—by tracking ALL your time spent for each client—for at least three months.

You may find that your flat fees are bringing in, say, $75/hour for some clients, and $25/hour for one or two clients.

This discovery will give you both the guts and the ammunition to go to those time-intensive clients and explain why you have to raise their prices. You can say your flat rates are priced to earn you $75 an hour. After review, you've found you've badly underestimated the time required for their account, and you are only receiving $25/hour. That's why you must triple the price for the next project.

Naturally the client will protest. But you should stand firm. Why should this client pay just 1/3 of what other clients are perfectly willing to pay? Couldn't you use the time spent on this client more profitably? Such as use it to solicit new clients who will pay your full rate?

One last-ditch way this client may try to talk you out of this: They may promise to require less time from you in the future. If they use this tactic, offer to work for them on an hourly basis, at your $75 per hour. This may work, if your client really believes they can require less hand-holding. But . . . the client may have no intention of demanding less from you—they just want to keep you working for them at 1/3 of your market value. If they refuse the hourly option, you should strongly consider dropping them. Or, offer to do jobs for them only sporadically, if and when you have down time.

As long as you are covering your expenses, you may be surprised at the benefits you receive from dropping a client such as this. Even if your new sales efforts don't land new clients, you may enjoy more quality time with the family—or just relaxing. And you may find that downtime gets you new ideas for new products or new marketing programs, or other new ways you could increase your earnings.

It's hard to come up with new ideas when your nose is pressed to the grindstone, and you're just trying to make deadlines. You need time for your brain to become more creative.

PART II

HOW TO RAISE PRICES — WITHOUT
CHANGING ANYTHING ELSE

Some tactics for increasing prices require nothing more from you than to just bump up the price!

The tactics in this section, will require no changes to the product, no changes to the promotion, distribution, or anything else.

You'll find the ideas in this section are the easiest in this book to test, rollout, and profit from.

2

Move your price up to the next "barrier"

There are psychological barriers in prices you must recognize. Particularly risky is increasing the number on the <u>farthest left</u> of your price. Riskiest of all is moving your price up another digit. For example, moving from 1 digit ($9) to 2 digits ($10), or from 2 digits ($99) to 3 ($100.)

All of these moves up over a barrier are likely to result in a large drop in your units sold.

Examples:

- Moving from $9 to $10 (AND . . . it adds a digit)
- Moving from $19 to $20
- Moving from $29 to $30
- Moving from $99 to $100 (AND . . . it adds a digit)
- Moving from $999 to $1,000 (Another added digit)

What does this mean for you if you want to RAISE prices? It means you can often raise your price right up to that barrier without experiencing any drop in sales.

Examples:

- Your price is $9. You can probably increase it to $9.99 without a drop in sales. Why? Your price is already $9. Adding some cents to it—as long as it doesn't go over $10—may well go unnoticed by customers.
- Your price is $19.50. You can probably increase it to $19.99 without a drop in sales.

Note that this does NOT mean if your price is $17, you can raise it to $19.99 —because you haven't gone over the $20 barrier. There could be another barrier going from $17 to $18. Or from $18 to $19. You can only find out if those other barriers are there by testing prices.

- Your price is $190. You can probably move to $199 with no loss in sales.
- Your price is $9,500. You can probably move it to $9,750 or even $9,950 without losing sales.

Warning about this tactic

You will notice my frequent use of "probably" above. That's because it is always dangerous to change prices without testing. Sometimes responses will change in unpredictable ways.

This tactic is likely to work for you. But . . . you may be unlucky enough to have customers who do not react in this expected manner. There are exceptions to every rule.

When testing money and lists are limited, I have often recommended to small clients that they just go ahead with these changes. And pay attention to results afterwards, just in case there is a problem.

However, for companies with large lists and adequate funding, I always recommend testing any price change before implementing it.

#3

Reduce the level of discounts you offer

There is credible research that shows a negative effect on sales for the higher levels of discounts—that offering a higher discount may actually REDUCE the number of buyers!

However, there is other research showing that discounts so high they are implausible—e.g., 70% off!—will still attract more buyers than lower discounts.

Since it would be wonderful to be able to lower your discounts—and get MORE buyers at a HIGHER price—this chapter will look at this research to see:

1. Why there are contradictions, and
2. How you can best use this knowledge

Why the research differs

Many marketing researchers have studied consumer reaction to various discount levels and found different results. However, here are some reasons why their results don't agree:

1. Different products: Researchers selected different products for their research, which might have different results due to:

- Different price points
- Different risks associated with different products

2. Different sale environments: Some researchers have studied responses to discount levels at high-end retail stores, some at discount retail stores and some on Internet stores.

3. Different consumers: There may be different responses to discount levels due to buyer gender, age, or income levels

In 2004, I did a study with Dr. Ronald Drozdenko that looked at the effects of discount levels on purchase intention and quality perceptions. This study tried to account for all the different variables above which might have been causing confusing responses.

We found that, over all the products we studied, there was a drop-off moving from a 30% discount to a 45% discount in both the buyer's perception of the quality of the product as well as in their intent to buy.

**Intent to Purchase & Quality Perceptions
at Different Discount Levels
(Rated from *1-10* where *10* is the highest)**

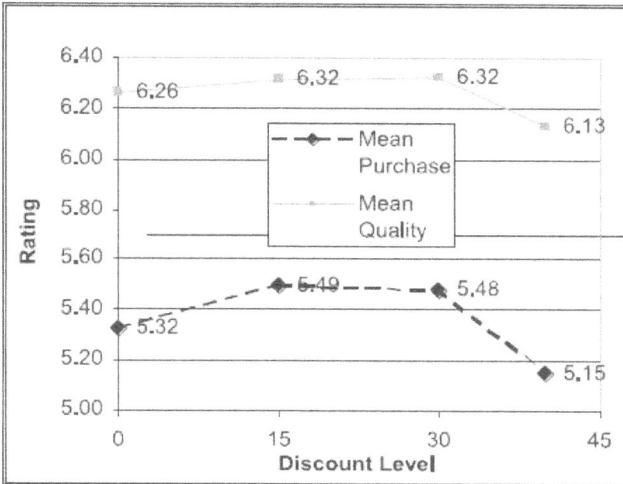

We further found (see chart above) that known brands can offer higher discount levels than unknown brands. Known brands had the highest quality levels and intent to purchase at the 30% discount level —higher than the above levels. Unknown brands dropped off on both rankings after the 15% discount level.

Effect of known brand name on quality perceptions & intent-to-purchase

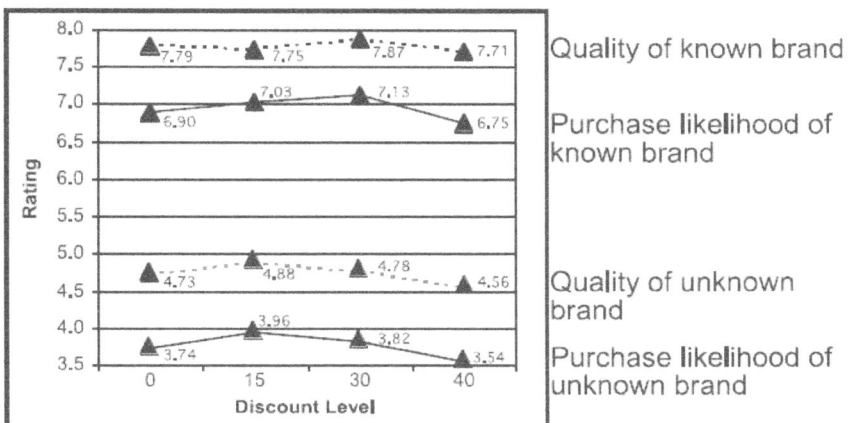

This means that if you are a new company or new product, you need to worry about any discount level over 15% — because it may cause buyers to doubt your quality and decrease their likelihood to buy.

Types of products where discounts should not be high

Later in 2004, Dr. Drozdenko and I conducted another study where we asked consumers to tell us their maximum acceptable discount for a number of different products, including athletic shoes, tires, shirts, toothpaste, a large screen HDTV, cereal, shampoo and watches.

For each product, we told them to assume it was a name brand, and gave them a list price. Consumers could select from a chart going from a 10% discount up to an 80% discount.

Results?

- Only 13% of all consumers selected the highest discount (80%) for each product. Thus, where consumers could choose—and see the actual reduced price for each discount level—87% of them chose to pay a price that was HIGHER than needed!
- Discounts from Internet retailers caused more concern than discounts from bricks & mortar stores.
- Lower income customers were more attracted to higher discount levels, as were younger customers.
- Consumers were most concerned about high discounts with tires.
- Consumers were 2nd most concerned about high discounts with cereal.
- Consumers were least concerned about high discounts with shirts.

Why would consumers choose to pay more?

After they made their choices, we asked those consumers why they accepted less than the maximum for some (or all) products. Here are their reasons:

- 54% Worried about the quality
- 51% Worried the products may be damaged
- 46% Worried the products may be outdated
- 43% Worried the products may be old
- 33% Worried the products may be knock-offs
- 24% Worried the products may be stolen

What does it mean?

What does it all mean for your ability to raise prices? If you are currently offering high discounts (30% or higher, especially 45% or higher), test whether you should reduce the level of your discounts under the following situations:

- You sell products where there is a safety risk (e.g., tires)
- You sell products where there is a freshness/staleness risk (e.g., cereal)
- Your target customers are over 30.
- Your target customers are relatively affluent.
- Your brand is mostly unknown.
- Your sales are mostly over the Internet.

Exceptions:

If your industry (e.g., e-books and software) or market (e.g., Singapore) typically has higher discounts, buyers may be conditioned to accept them as normal.

4

Raise your price only for the "initial" buy

If your product or service is delivered over time, the initial buy is when your customers are the most committed to you. The most motivated. The most eager to receive what you supply.

Therefore, there is no time when a higher price is as acceptable.

Psychologically, people are more likely to focus on follow-up payments—the monthly cost—than on a one-time "initiation fee."

Raise your entrance fee

If you have a membership website, a club or an association, there are two kinds of entrance fees you can charge, depending on whether you charge by the month or by the year. Raising the price of the entrance fee is less likely—depending upon your competitive situation—to cause sales drop off than raising the continuing monthly or annual fee:

1. **Monthly billing:** You charge an initial—higher—fee for the first month, then a lower fee for every following month.

2. **Annual billing:** You charge an annual fee for membership and—in the first month only—you charge an initiation fee.

Other methods for increasing your initial profits

Magazines and newsletters utilize this same psychology by offering a "renewal at birth." When someone orders an annual subscription, they send the bill with an extra choice on it: The new subscriber can pay their bill for a 1-year subscription, or they can pay for a 2-year subscription, with a discount on the 2nd-year price as their reward.

The psychology behind this offer is that the buyer is most likely to be committed at the moment they've made the buying decision. They're excited about receiving the publication, so they're in an optimal frame of mind for adding on another year to their purchase.

Because they offer a discount on the 2nd year price, you may believe that this tactic works against the premise of this book—raising prices. But when you look at the net cash per subscriber, this tactic almost always increases it.

Publications have a serious drop-off in subscribers at the point of first renewal. Consumer publications can lose up to 75% of their first year subscribers at renewal time. *[Note: After a subscriber has renewed once, the vast majority of them are likely to continue renewing in the future.]*

Therefore, a tactic which delivers 85-90% of a full year's price for the second year—when most of those subscribers would have paid nothing—is a tactic that increases your revenue per subscriber and your profits.

5

Raise your "hidden" prices

Do you have a schedule or menu of prices (called non-linear pricing)? That is, a number of different prices depending on what configuration your customer buys?

Examples:

When buying magazine advertising, there are different rates for all of the following:

- Magazines sell advertising with a full menu of prices. Prices vary depending on the size of the ad, how many ads are bought, and whether they are full color, 2-color or B&W.
- Other industries often have at least volume discounts, but may also have price schedules for different configurations of their product or service.

If you have this non-linear pricing, there are two excellent opportunities for getting price increases:

How to get a bigger increase than you announce

Often in markets with a menu of prices, there are one (or two or three) specific prices most closely watched by the marketplace.

Announcement example:

Publications selling advertising are expected, each year, to announce the next year's rate increase. That announcement has traditionally been the rate for running a single full ad page at either the B&W or 4-Color rate. Further, because magazines all have different circulation which would make comparison for ad buyers cumbersome, the rate is announced as an increase in the CPM (cost per thousand readers). Thus you'll see announcements that the 1X 4-C CPM will rise by 6% (for example).

However, there are literally hundreds of additional prices which are not, by tradition, required to be announced. The assumption is that those rate increases are roughly the same as the announced rate increases.

Many publications have made a fortune by not raising all rates uniformly. Thus they could announce a 6% rate increase, and actually profit from a 9% rate increase—averaged over all their business at all their different prices.

How to analyze your price list for hidden opportunities

The key to successfully wringing out the maximum amount of profit from your menu of prices is to know exactly how much business is in each of your "cells." If you don't know that, you are just fumbling around in the dark.

Example of the "cells" of a price schedule
(Showing annual revenues received for each cell)

	Basic model	Basic + A	Basic + A&B	Premium model
1-5 units bought	$100K	$1K	$125K	$260K
6-15 units bought	$5K	$50K	$150K	$15K
16-30 units bought	$20K	$60K	$250K	$0
31-50 units bought	$28K	$10K	$25K	$10K
51+ units bought	$210K	$0	$240K	$120K

In this example, this company offers 4 different versions of its product, and also offers 5 different price breaks for each model—depending upon the quantity purchased. Inside each cell you will see the annual revenue the company receives from customers who are paying that specific price. *(Total company revenue in this example is: $1.7 million.)*

The reason for this elaborate example is to show that many of these cells produce no sales at all—or minimal sales. If you raise those specific prices an extra amount—it will be worthless to your bottom line.

On the other hand, in this example, there are four cells each producing over $200,000 in revenue *(shown in bold)*. If you increased your 6% rate increase to an 8% rate increase in ONLY those 4 cells, you would pocket an extra $192K in annual profits. Even if you could only increase those 4 cells by an extra 1%, you would still have an extra $96K PROFIT per year.

Additional pricing insights from this analysis

Notice in the "Basic + A" column above that this company has much lower sales of this model, relative to the others. Thus, raising the price on this model will not earn the company nearly as much as raising it on one of the other models.

Further, if you look at the "16-30 units bought" row, you will see that few of this company's customers are using the volume discount for 16-30 units. Again, this tells you that raising that rate will earn the company far less than raising the rate for one of the other volume discount levels.

However . . . consider what might happen if you left this rate, but gave a bigger price increase to the 6-15 units rate. You might be able to entice those buyers to buy more units to qualify for the 16-30 rate.

Doing this analysis is critical for businesses with menu (non-linear) pricing. Only through this exercise can you clearly see the leverage points in your business. Once you know where these points are in your pricing menu, you will make much smarter pricing decisions.

6

Increase prices for high-demand segments only

Paying more for "peak time" usage is something almost expected by consumers. And "peak time" is by definition used by those customers who are least price sensitive.

You are more likely to be able to raise prices to this group—with no falloff in customers—than to those customers who are buying at non-peak times, thus exhibiting a potential price sensitivity.

Examples of businesses which segment customers into "high-demand time" and "low-demand time":

- Trains (commuter trains charge more for traveling during rush hour)
- Electricity suppliers (higher rates during the evening, or during summer?)
- Airlines (higher rates for holiday travel)
- Hotels (higher rates "in-season" than "off-season")
- Restaurants (higher rates for dinner than for lunch)

How you can segment for "high-demand"

Don't assume that time of day is the only segment that can break out high-demand customers. Or assume that this tactic only works for utilities. See if one of the ideas below could work for your business.

Time periods of high demand

This is the most common segmentation for high-demand customers, and yet it's not as used as it could be. Many people are leaving money on the table by not considering whether they could add a premium to people seeking their product or service at a particular time.

Example:

Hair salons could give a price break for early in the week appointments, since more (women, anyway) wish to have their hair done on Friday or Saturday.

Seasons of high demand

Times of the year can also create more high-demand customers. For example, hotels in the Caribbean cost more in the winter than in the summer. Again, this is something more companies could take advantage of.

Example:

Tax accountants could increase their prices by 15%, then give a discount for those who contact you in January or February. Or before March 6th. Whatever works for you. Anyone seeking your service after that time does not qualify for your discount.

High-demand customer types

Segmentation can also be done by types of customers, although this is a little trickier. You can't discriminate on price between two customers who are roughly the same. But you can discriminate when there is a difference that you can use to justify different prices.

Examples:

Airlines: Airlines segment by customer types, charging a premium for business travelers. The tricky part in setting up this price segmentation was determining how to identify a business vs. a personal traveler. If airlines asked, smart customers would all say "personal" to get the lower rates. Instead, airlines selected a pattern of booking early vs. booking late which allows them to identify a high percentage of business travelers—and sock them with a premium price.

Airlines are a good example, also, of how this tactic can backfire if you create too large a distance between prices for your two groups. With a huge price difference, this tactic encourages new competitors to enter the market. In the airline industry, the result was small commuter airlines jumping from 5% of the market to over 20% of the market in just a few years.

Emergency fix-it services: You don't get more high demand than a person who has locked themselves out of the car—or their home. And the prices charged by locksmiths who make "house calls" (or car calls!) are breathtakingly, and appropriately, high.

The same holds for auto glass firms. Come in and pay price X to have your cracked window shield replaced. Or rest in the comfort of your home while paying more to have someone come fix it in your driveway.

Baby sitting: Baby sitters are allowed to have a life, and a schedule, of their own. If a customer contracts ahead of time, they could get a discounted rate. If they want service at the last minute—why not charge a premium?

7

Make "unnoticeable" price increases

You will have difficulty using this tactic if:

1. If you sell exactly the same product & features as do your competitors (see other chapters in this book on how to avoid this!), AND
2. Your products are sold in a retail store or over the Internet, where customers can easily compare prices, AND
3. You're an unknown brand

Everyone else has a good chance of finding price-raising opportunities here.

Are certain price differences "unnoticeable"?

Consumers usually do not see your prices as a complete surprise. They may already have a rough idea of what your price is, or at least what prices for your type of product/service generally run. This is called an *"internal* reference price."

Or, they may have seen prices in ads, or be looking at prices marked on store shelves. Those are *"external reference prices."*

There are two marketing theories that suggest consumers are looking for your price to be within a certain RANGE—instead of expecting an exact price.

- *Assimilation-contrast theory* holds that consumers accept prices within their internal reference price range, and reject those outside the range.
- *Range theory* holds that consumers use the highest and lowest points of their expected price range for your category as signals within which they evaluate your price.

How wide a price range are you likely to get? An interesting study by Kalyanaram & Little [*Journal of Marketing Research, 21(3)*] found consumers buying sweetened and unsweetened drinks in a supermarket had a price range of 1.5 times the price variability. That means if unsweetened drinks for sale in the supermarket varied from $.99 to $1.29, then the consumer reference price range would be $.45 (1.5 times $.30).

I wouldn't recommend you count on this calculation, especially for different product types. But it did show a surprisingly large range within which consumers are much less price sensitive.

The authors also found that the more knowledgeable the buyer was about the product category, the smaller their acceptable range. And that brand-loyal customers had a wider range, perhaps judging all other brand prices from the starting point of their favorite brand.

In a separate research study, Kalwani & Yim concluded:

"We find evidence in support of a region of price insensitivity around a brand's expected price within which price changes do not produce a significant change in consumers' price perceptions."

(Journal of Marketing Research, February 1992)

Their findings reinforce a conclusion by Gurumurthy & Little (in a MIT working paper) that was memorably phrased:

"Marketers wishing to increase prices should nibble, not bite."

What does this mean for YOU?

If consumers have an expected price range, and are relatively insensitive to any price within that range, you should be able to raise your prices as long as you don't raise them enough to move them out of the expected range.

Therein lies a problem: How do you know what their expected range is?

You can find that through price testing, of course, or through conjoint studies. However, some companies, especially those where price testing is expensive, reserve price testing for large price differences.

Some companies try testing the limits of an expected price range by trial and error. They bump their price up a little and see if it affects sales. If not, they may bump it again in 3-6 months and again see what happens.

Sometimes, if you sell in multiple channels, you can bump up the price in an easy-to-test and practically-no-cost environment (e.g., the Internet) and get an early reading, before rolling it out across the board. If a tested price doesn't work on the Internet, it is very easy to change it back.

So . . . If your price is currently $16.50, could you move it to $16.99 without exceeding the consumer price range? Probably. But don't forget what you learned in the chapter on barrier pricing: If your price is $19.99, it is unlikely you can go up even a penny without it being noticeable.

8

Break out some fees previously included in your price

Suppose your price is $99, and you haven't been able to raise prices over $100. If you have included the cost of more than just your one product or service in your price, you can unbundle the components of the price and then raise one of them.

Example:

You have a B2B newsletter which is priced at $399/year, which includes the distribution (postage) of that newsletter. You could test continuing to price your newsletter at $399/year, but add in a $10/year delivery fee on top of it. That fee would be added in at the checkout, along with any sales taxes you are required to collect.

That way, there could still be a stumbling block when the amount is totaled up, but it is likely to result in fewer lost sales than an initial price of $409 in your promotion materials.

Example:

If you provide business software which requires substantial training of employees before they can utilize it, you could break out the price for the in-person training from the package. Thus the software price looks less intimidating and the training part of what you deliver is shown at its substantial value.

Everyone loves a bargain

Let's make sure we all learn from amazon.com, however, when we look at shipping costs on orders. Amazon.com first tried a "free shipping" option when a competitor offered the same. They liked the results so much that they kept it with particular "rules" that determined whether a buyer could qualify.

- You had to buy at least $25
- Of goods that could go in the same box
- And agree to a slower delivery

Because amazon.com's free shipping option results in a loss to amazon.com of $3 (or more) per order—there must be some very compelling reason(s) for continuing the promotion — and even expanding it today to eliminate many of those "conditions."

I can think of only two possible compelling reasons:

1. More people are buying
2. The dollar amount of the average order has risen

How can you use both this tactic and amazon's?

Breaking out shipping costs—or some other expenses connected with the delivery of your product or service—can be a price increase tactic. You leave your basic price the same and add on the shipping/other fees.

However, today Amazon has spoiled much of America into expecting no shipping costs. And online retailers know they often lose customers when they look at the shipping costs when checking out.

So... offer your buyers some way to avoid the extra shipping/delivery fees, for an order size or dollar value that is over your "average."

This combined strategy would give you:

- Extra money from those paying the shipping fee
- Extra sales from those trying to increase their order size to avoid the fee

9

Offer discounts—after raising your list price

Raising your prices, then offering especially price sensitive buyers a way to offset that increase can be one of the smartest price-only changes you can make. (Although be cautious about discounting when you sell a luxury product or service.)

Following are some types of discounts that have been offered by companies. One or more of them could fit your customer base very well. Note: Many come from B2B sales, but don't automatically assume they won't work for consumer sales. Think about each and see if there's a way it could be adapted to what you sell and your customers—or potential customers.

WARNING: Don't get all excited about these different discounts and go implementing one or more—WITHOUT FIRST RAISING YOUR BASE PRICE! Remember your goal, the reason you bought this book, is to be able to raise prices—not lower them.

If you raise prices by 10%, but give your most price sensitive customers a way to get a 10% discount if they follow certain rules for the discount—you've removed much of the anger about the price raise. You've made the increase go away—IF the customer qualifies for the discount.

Thus your customers will sort themselves into these groups:

1. Groups where you get higher price

- Price INsensitive customers who don't care about the higher price
- Price sensitive customers who don't qualify for your discount(s)

2. Groups where you get the same prices, but possibly higher volume

- Price sensitive customers who make sure they qualify for the discount
- Price INsensitive customers who qualify for discounts and take them as long as they are easy to get

Alternatively, you can use this chapter to look at discounts you can reduce or remove. Getting rid of discounts you already offer carries the same effect as raising your prices!

Volume discounts

Volume discounts come in two forms:

1. Discounts for the size of a single order, or
2. Annual volume discounts, available based on total purchases over a full year.

Which should you offer? Offer #1 if you save money in fulfilling one large order vs. several small ones. Otherwise, choose whichever you think would work best for you and your customers. Obviously there is a little more paperwork involved if you base discounts on annual volume instead of individual order size. But . . . there could be an incentive for your customers to buy more near year end if they're close to another discount level.

Price-barrier discounts

These are discounts available only to customers who spend above a fixed amount. An example is a retail store eliminating shipping costs if you spend above $25.

Increased-buying discounts

These are great for signing up new customers—without alienating your current customers. Anything a new customer buys is, by definition, an increase from their purchases the previous year—so they qualify for the discount. But current customers who increase their sales with you by 10% or 15% or whatever your discount levels are—also qualify.

These are good discounts to use when your goals are both to develop new buyers and to steal business from competitors.

Exclusivity or competitive discounts

These discounts reward buyers who buy only from you or buyers who increase the share you get of their total buying. They're offered for competitive reasons, to block a new competitor or to increase your share-of-market relative to current competitors. I don't believe this discount is applicable for B2C, but you may be smarter than me and know how to apply it to B2C. If so, please let me know at Jensen at PricingPsychology dot com!

Customer pick-up discounts

This discount represents a removed shipping charge available to those who pick up their purchases at some location convenient to the seller.

Quick-pay or cash-with-order discounts

These are offered in both consumer and B2B sales. In B2B, the discount is usually stated as 2/10, meaning if you pay within 10 days you can take off a 2% discount.

The problem with these discounts, is that your customers who do not pay quickly often try to take them as well.

In B2C, companies that bill have found a premium available for cash-with-order is generally better than a discount—and often costs less as well.

In B2B, many companies have thrown in the towel and eliminated this discount rather than get into unpleasant situations with customers trying to claim it without qualifying for it.

Co-op advertising discounts

These are discounts, usually up to 1-2% of a retail store's total purchases from you, for advertising they run which includes your product along with their store as the place to buy it.

Again, this discount is probably not applicable in B2C, but it would work in more B2B markets than are currently using it.

Extended-payment plans

Allowing someone to pay over a longer-than-normal period of time, is really offering them a discount.

In B2B, it is seen as a discount or buying incentive.

In B2C, it is the only way some people can buy your product. More consumers than the government wants to acknowledge are living paycheck to paycheck. For those people, the amount they pay per month is more important than the amount they pay in total. For example, which of the following offers is more attractive:

1. A living room furniture set for $1,250, or
2. A living room furniture set for $1,750, which you can pay for at $250/month?

There are a large number of customers who would prefer #2 above.

10

Offer coupons, after raising your list price

Coupons are another useful method of not scaring away price sensitive customers, while still getting higher prices from those not price sensitive.

Again, the idea is to raise your base price, then offer coupons that lower it to those willing to seek out and clip coupons.

If you're worried enough about customers not finding your coupons, you could even reference coupon locations. Such as:

- Don't miss our discount coupons available in your local Sunday paper.
- Check out our discount coupons at www.smartsource.com , www.groupon.com, (or wherever you have them on the Internet).

However, do not have discount coupons on your website for offers on your website. Coupons directly on your website should only be good for redemption in a physical store. If you only sell electronically, put your coupons on a different site, preferably a coupon-type site, where the visitor will have to search a little for them.

Otherwise you make it too easy, and every buyer will use one. Only by adding in a couple of steps—before coupons can be used—do you cause buyers to segment themselves into price sensitive and price insensitive groups.

And only when buyers divide themselves into those two groups will you get the full price from those who don't care enough about saving the money to take those extra steps.

11

Offer rebates, after raising your list price

Rebates work the same as coupons, except for three differences:

1. Rebates come AFTER the purchase
2. Rebates are usually for bigger dollar amounts
3. Rebates make you jump through more hoops than do coupons

Coupons, usually for no more than a dollar discount, are easier to get and use than rebates. That's because even a tiny bit of bother will stop a price insensitive buyer from following through—just to save pennies.

However, when the savings is $20 (or a similar large amount), most people will take an extra step or two to get the discount—even those with lots of money.

That's why rebates include more than a step or two:

- First you have to buy the product at full price.
- Then you have to cut out product codes from the box

- Then you have to fill out a rebate slip.
- You have to make copies of your sales slip and the filled out info.
- You have to dig up an envelope, write in their address & your return address, and put it all in the mail. (Or go to a specific website to enter everything.)
- Then you have to keep it in a follow-up place, because some rebate companies have been scams, and you have to be prepared to demand your rebate if the 8 weeks go by without it being received.
- You also have to be willing to put up with the psychological stress of knowing you could do all this work and still have to fight the company because you never got the rebate.

Faced with all the above hassle, only those who are most determined to get the lower price will follow through.

One of the great things about rebates (in addition to all those people who don't file for it!) is that you can use the discounted price on your packaging.

Your price on your package can say: **$99 (after $20 rebate)** instead of saying: **$119**

This allows you to promote the product at the lower, after-rebate price, while still getting a $20 price increase on all those who don't do the paperwork.

Although you do have to hire a firm to process rebates, a "price increase" just doesn't get any easier—or less noticeable—than this!

#12

Test higher prices

If there's only one technique you use from this book, it should be this one. Test! Test! Test!

Each market is different and you may find interesting—and very profitable—prices that appeal to your market.

However, it is much harder—although not impossible—to test prices if:

- You sell only in physical retail stores, or
- You sell very high priced equipment in B2B

Critical for high-quality products and personal services

Testing is even more critical if your product or service is positioned as high-quality, or if you sell services where customers cannot easily ascertain the quality of what you provide (e.g., legal, financial, tax services, plastic surgery, etc.).

That's because a higher price will almost always convey a higher quality to potential buyers. Example: a psychologist said that she raised her rates and could not believe the number of new customers that she received. Her clients perceived she was a better psychologist because her rates were higher.

Testing higher prices via direct response

Direct response (via mail, e-mail, websites, or telephone) is the gold standard of price testing. You can TRUST the results you get. That's because you can:

- Make your offers identical except for the price
- Randomize who receives each offer

In mail, you divide the list into three RANDOMIZED groups—to test three prices

On a website, you use software, such as Google AdWords or Analytics, so that (again testing three prices), visitor #1 sees price #1, visitor #2 sees price #2, visitor #3 sees price #3, visitor #4 sees price #1, etc.

- Make sure your mailing lists are big enough, or your Internet test runs long enough that you get at least 40 orders into your winning group.

If you sell in retail stores, but also on the Internet, you can test prices on the Internet only. That gives you the Gold Standard testing, but it doesn't address possible differences by region of the country, nor possible differences among people who don't use the Internet.

Price testing when you can't use direct response

Please don't use some "research" that asks potential buyers what price they would be willing to pay! Allow me to quote from my book *The Tao of Pricing:*

> Asking buyers what they're willing to pay
> is like asking a fox to guard your henhouse.
> Why, then, trust survey responses to set prices?
> ©2019 www.TaoOfPricing.com

The only research that can give you reliable pricing answers is something called Choice-Based Conjoint (CBC). You need a professional researcher to conduct and analyze this research for you —preferably a researcher from a price consulting company. The leading price-consulting firms are members of the Professional Pricing Society and you can search their experts database at: www.pricingsociety.com.

CBC allows you to pair different prices with different offers, product configurations, or other variables. This is important because it gives you additional information—and prevents the research from being easily seen through. Thus you might have 5 prices, 3 configurations (additional features added to the product), 4 colors, etc.

Earlier conjoint analysis had respondents rank their choices from 1-10, but that is not how buyers act in the real world. CBC takes them closer to the real world model.

Respondents will get a series of choices. For example:

Choice #1: If you wanted to buy an HDTV, and these were your only choices, which of these would you buy?

- HDTV with a 3 year warranty, 30" for $2,250
- HDTV with a 1 year warranty, 26" for $1,950
- HTTV with a 3 year warranty, 26" for $2,100
- None of the 3

The software takes all your variables and pairs them into just 10-20 choices of 3-4 options (plus none), then is able to draw conclusions on all the variables.

In addition to actual pricing for the configuration you planned, CBC will tell you, in this example, what dollar value buyers put on a longer warranty, and on a bigger sized screen.

#13

Add a cushion (or bigger one) to all your bids for jobs

The intent of this book is to prevent you from losing sales when you raise your prices, but this particular tactic is likely to cost you some jobs.

However, it may also raise your profits!

The "Winner's Curse"

If you bid competitively for jobs, you must factor in a number of subjective estimates on how long the job will take, how demanding the client will be, and possibly how big a local regulatory problem you are likely to encounter. Many of these factors are impossible to really know before you start doing the job.

Let's say you are bidding against 5 other firms, each roughly as qualified as your company. Each of the companies must also estimate the cost to them of these subjective factors. Each comes up with a bid.

Your bid is lowest—so you get the job. Congratulations! Or . . . maybe you should instead be offered condolences?

Unless you have company assets that allow you to perform the job for a lower price than your competitors (maybe you own a lumber company?), the reason your bid is lowest is likely to be your evaluation of the subjective—impossible to know up front—factors. Your four competitors have evaluated the cost of those factors higher than you did. Maybe they know something you don't? Maybe they know working in this town is incredibly difficult. Maybe they know you have to bribe someone to get permits through? Maybe they know the client is impossible?

The point is that sometimes the reason you are the lowest bidder is because you underestimated what your real costs are going to be. Which means that this job won't earn you the profit you expected. It could even lose money for your company.

Hence the expression—"winner's curse."

What is the solution?

The solution is to add a cushion, or a larger cushion, to protect you against inadvertently underestimating some of the costs of the job.

The result is likely to be fewer jobs that you "win." This could hurt your profits. Or, if you have occasionally been stung by underestimating the costs of a job, it could save you from "winning" a job at a price that will lose money for your company. The net result would then be an overall price increase—because those jobs you do win will be more profitable.

Obviously, the problem is knowing how much of a cushion will protect you without losing you profitable jobs. That question, however, could fill an entire book on its own—and still not give you a dependable answer! Experience—and trial and error—are likely to be your best solution.

#14

Just Do It(!)

As you can see from the different tactics in this Part II, it matters very much what number you use for your increased price. A 5% increase that results in a price of $40 will be much less acceptable to your customers than a 9% increase that results in a price of $39.99. The percent increase is clearly less important than the final price number.

And... price testing allows you to fine tune your prices even better — to hit the perfect sweet spot with your customers.

However, service businesses may still hesitate. You typically have far fewer customers, can't afford to lose any, and often can't do reliable price testing.

This tactic is for you!

Raise them and see what happens

Yes, it's that simple. Raise them and see if anyone complains. Don't announce them. Don't apologize for them. Just do it.

You may be shocked that nobody says anything to you and just pays the new higher price without comment. In fact, most entrepreneurs are too afraid to charge what their product/service is really worth.

If nobody complains, wait a few months then raise them again. Do this until you finally get real pushback on a price increase. Only then have you reached the price that reflects the value your customers perceive in your product or service.

Just remember to keep pricing psychology in mind as you select your number. If you're at $350, and you want to try $400 — be smart and come in at $395 or $399 instead.

PART III

PRODUCT CHANGES THAT LET YOU RAISE PRICES

Some of the best price-raising tactics require a change to the product or service you are selling.

Sometimes the changes are small; other times large.

Regardless, a product change that can increase your profit margins is a product change to be considered.

#15

Increase value in your "package" with added features

What makes up your product or service? Are there additions you can make to it, to increase its value to your customers?

Sometimes the cost to you of adding highly-valued features is minimal. The catch is—you need to know what features are truly valued, and which are just "nice" but don't convey extra value in the customer's mind. The features you want to add are those that make it worth a higher price to your customer.

Bad example: Cheap multi-vitamin companies which promote they now have CoQ10 in them. Yes, this allows those companies to raise their prices. But . . . CoQ10 is an extremely expensive ingredient, and the amount added by these low-end vitamin companies is too small for your body to even notice it, much less benefit from it.

Good example: The addition of aloe to lotions. Aloe is not very expensive, yet the perceived value to consumers is high.

Getting real, statistically reliable answers

What features are valued at what price is exactly the question you can ask with a wonderful research tool that's been developed and standardized over the last 10-15 years. It's called CBC (Choice-Based Conjoint).

This research can take your base product or service and test 5-20 "additions" to it, and put a value-tag (like a price tag) on each of them. Thus you can know that adding X to your product or service makes it worth $20 more (or $2,000 more) in your customers' minds.

Basically, customers are offered choices. Here's a product with these features at this cost. Would you buy it or this same product with these other features at this different price? Or would you buy neither? The customer is offered 10-20 choices between three or four items. Based upon the answers, the software can extrapolate a value for each of the features.

Warning: Don't get talked into conjoint analysis that is not choice-based. There has been substantial literature in the last 15 years showing that choice based is more valid and more predictive of actual behavior than the alternatives, which have the customer ranking items. Choice-based is more real world—because that's how we buy: Do I select this or that?

If you do most business over the Internet, there is a module that allows you to send test subjects to a particular web page, where they can take the "test." Thus, this research can be conducted 100% online. Or offline.

What will it cost?

If you're a researcher

If you have a strong research background, and are selling multiple products, you might want to invest in this software yourself. The only company I can recommend is CBC Conjoint, from Sawtooth Software (www.SawToothSoftware.com).

Do NOT buy a conjoint package from other vendors as they are typically not choice-based, nor will they let you pull out results by different demographics to see if, for example, men have different values than women.

If you want professionals to do it for you

There are a number of pricing consultants who can conduct this research for you. You can find them at www.PricingSociety.com.

If money is tight

You may be able to get marketers or marketing students at your local college to conduct the research for you—as long as they can write up the results in a professional journal. However, CBC is still relatively new, and you may find many colleges don't have it or don't have anyone who's really worked with it. But it's worth a try.

If you can't afford it

If you can't afford to use conjoint analysis, there are some other ways of testing the value your customers put on different features. Unfortunately, they require a little more trial and error research.

Professional services: Offer two or three different versions of your services, each with an added benefit and an added price. Example: Monthly bookkeeping = $xxx. Monthly bookkeeping with payroll = $yyy. Monthly bookkeeping with tax returns = $zzz.

The problem with this test is that you have to assign the dollar value to each of the added services. Which means you could get it wrong. What if nobody buys the service (above) with the payroll addition? Does that mean they have payroll done elsewhere and aren't interested? Or that your added price is too high?

Product vendors: If you sell products, you can get much better results testing them on the Internet, even if you do more sales in your physical store(s).

If you already have a website selling your product, and if you devote an entire page to it, you can use Google Analytics to test different versions of that page. Each version would look the same, but would sell a different configuration of that same product—at a different price. If you were testing three versions, your first person to click on that page would see version A. The second person to click on that page would see version B. The third would see version C. The fourth would see version A. And so on.

If you don't have a setup where this would work, or if you aren't getting much traffic yet to your website, you can also test with Google's PPC AdWords program. [To learn more, go to www.adwords.google.com.]

You would create three (or however many versions you want to test) different ads that would run for the same keywords. Thus if you were selling custom birdcages, you would select that as your keyword. Your three ads would each say "custom birdcages" in the title, but in the small amount of copy below it would add in whatever features you wanted to test. Below is an example of one of the possible ads, where you wanted to see if adding a custom cover would add value in the minds of your consumers. In this case, you would vary ONLY the copy in italics:

Custom Birdcages
Unique birdcages—*with custom covers as well*—for reasonable prices.

Each of the ads you design would then link to a different page. On these ads, everything would be the same except for the added feature you're testing and the different price.

Again, the problem would be that you have to guess as to what would be most valued.

As an alternative, you could test 5 ads with 5 different benefits, all at the same price. That would tell you which of the added benefits are most valued. Then you could test different prices for your product with the top one or two added features.

16

Add high-value, high-margin peripherals

If someone buys your product or service, are there other purchases that could enhance the value of what you've already sold them? Additions that carry a fatter profit margin than your original product or service? If so, you can add them and use their fat profit margins to provide you with, in effect, a price increase.

The most powerful examples of this tactic are peripheral products that are consumed in the act of using your product or service. Think razor blades for a razor or ink cartridges for a printer. But those are not the only opportunities to profits from this tactic.

Suppose you offer an income tax preparation service to people in the lower to middle income brackets. And, given competition from H&R Block, you find you are limited in the amount you can charge for this service. What other add-on services could you provide to your current customers?

1. Could you interest the higher income group of these people in a pre-year-end tax planning session? Something you could sell by warning your customers that some strategic tax-

saving measures have to occur by year end or they can't take advantage of them that year?

2. How about a "saving for college" strategy session? You help your customers figure out how best to tap all the resources and tax benefits available—to lower their out-of-pocket for this looming huge expense.

Suppose you sell:

- Sweaters. Can you add an "under" sweater, a shell or tank top, that goes great with one or more of your sweaters?
- Coca Cola. Could you add a line of "Coke" merchandise? (Oops! They already do.)
- Art. Could you also sell frames? Your art on T-shirts? Note cards?
- Freelance writing. Could you also sell yourself as a photographer? To your current customers?
- Electrician services? Could you also offer carpentry services? From subcontractors? (My electrician does.)
- Boots. Could you make a great purse that goes perfectly with the boots?
- Necklaces? Could you add earrings that complement the necklaces?
- Subscriptions to your newsletter or magazine? Could you also sell audio or in-person conferences? Books? Reports? DVDs?

As you can see, there are a lot of peripheral high-profit-margin products which can be added to a "base" product. No, this technique won't work for every marketer, but for those who can take advantage of it—the extra profit can make a big difference. Even if only 10-20% of your buyers add in the extra product — that's a lot of high-margin sales to fatten your profits.

17

Make comparison to your competitors more difficult

Thanks to the Internet, comparison price shopping is incredibly easy. That makes it very easy for a consumer to chose your competitor for even a small price difference. This is obviously bad for healthy bottom lines.

What can you do?

Prepare a chart on your competitors

The best way to analyze your opportunities is to first chart your competitors. EXACTLY what are they offering at what price?

For example, if you are a tax accountant, what exactly are your local competitors including in their flat fee? What aren't they?

If you provide other **services,** ask the same questions.

- Are your competitors bonded?
- Do they provide a guarantee? If so, what?
- Do they offer discounts for an ongoing contract? Of what

length?

- Who has the most (or the most impressive) testimonials?
- Subscription website? What exactly do your members get compared to your competitors' members?
- Cleaning service? Do your competitors clean microwaves? Windows?
- Writer? Do your competitors include photos? How many revisions? Proofreading?
- Restaurant? How different is your ambience?
- Garage service? Do you drop off customers at their job—and pick them up? Do you guarantee a completion time?

If you produce **products**, how do they differ from your competitors?

For example, my brother (and former partner) Harold Fann wrote a book called *Step-by-Step Websites in 3-6 Hours with Dreamweaver MX*. It was 120 pages and we sold it for $37. However, you could buy a book online called *Dreamweaver, the Missing Manual*. It was over 600 pages and sold for $24.46. Why would anyone spend more for less? Because what you were paying Harold for is the work he did that will let you AVOID having to read over 600 pages of technical stuff—to find the few pages of exactly what you need to create a website that will start earning you money on the Internet. All those extra pages can be positioned as a benefit. Or they can be positioned as a negative!

Books, however, have it much easier in differentiating products from competitors. What if you produce more close-to-identical products? Here are some questions you can ask:

- Guarantee differences? What could that mean to buyers?
- Differences in customer service? How could that matter?
- Differences in quality materials used in its manufacture?
- Differences in how it affects any of the senses? Tactile? Visual?
- Differences in prestige? Who is endorsing each?
- Differences in how easily you can buy the product? Does one of you have better distribution?

Use the chart to differentiate your product/service

Once you've carefully analyzed differences between your product/service and those of your competitors, you can then decide how to reposition your offering.

This is different from Tactic #15 (where you will look at adding high-value features to your product) and #16 (where you looked at selling additional, complementary products). Here we're just trying to make two roughly identical products or services NOT look like they're identical.

The results of this analysis could lead you to change an ad for your product from something such as:

[Brand name] does [benefit] for you!

To something like:

*The best guarantee makes [brand name]
the no-worry choice for [benefit]!*

Or: An ad that focuses on the positive attention you'll get from peers for your choice—which shows your product is not equal in perception among certain peer groups.

If your product/service is one where customers worry about its quality over time, just adding a year or two to your guarantee—and prominently featuring that difference—can make it more difficult for a consumer to evaluate your product relative to competitors.

For example: Which is the better buy? Product A with a 90-day guarantee at $49 or Product B with a full year's guarantee at $54? It depends, doesn't it? But the real key is the consumer is no longer comparing apples to apples.

Just make sure when your product is Googled or searched for that the differences between yours and your competitors' products/services are front and center.

#18

Spin off a luxury version of your product/service

Luxury versions do not only apply to watches and clothing. You can have a luxury candy bar, luxury ice cream, even luxury bottled water.

This obviously appeals to consumers who want the best of everything. But it can also appeal to lower-income people. Almost everyone can afford to splurge on a luxury candy bar. Or a luxury bubble bath packet. Look at the wonderful tag line for L'Oreal hair dye: "Because you're WORTH it!"

While this tactic doesn't increase the price of your base product, it does increase the average price you get for that category of products. And . . . your profit margin on this new version is likely to be much higher than for the base product.

Once you are set up to provide a product or service, your added costs to add a luxury version are likely to be small.

The best way to utilize this tactic is to add a high-value-to-your-customers component to your luxury version—a component which doesn't cost much to add.

However, sometimes elegant packaging and/or presentation by itself is almost enough difference between your "normal" and your "luxury" product.

19

Spin off a higher-priced model even if you know it will sell poorly

This tactic is best for companies which offer a line of product models —where some are cheaper and some are higher priced. And it's best illustrated with two examples.

Suppose your company sells ink jet printers. Let's say you have three models as listed below. I've made an estimate of what each model might contribute to your total ink jet printer sales.

BASE EXAMPLE
WITH % OF YOUR TOTAL INK JET PRINTER SALES

Model #1
$99.99
60%
Model #2
$129.99
30%
Model #3
$149.99
10%

NOW, SUPPOSE YOU CONSIDER ADDING A HIGHER-PRICED MODEL TO THIS grouping. And suppose you know it will not get more than 4% of your total sales.

Instead of making a snap decision that this is a bad move, you need to consider how that higher-priced model will affect the sales of your other models. In fact, you may well find yourself with results that look like the following:

NEW EXAMPLE

Model #1

$99.99

50%

Model #2

$129.99

27%

Model #3

$149.99

19%

New Model #4

$169.99

4%

WHY MIGHT ADDING MODEL #4 RAISE THE SALES OF YOUR MODEL #3, which was previously your highest-priced model?

Quite a few consumers will never buy the highest priced model of anything. They think it is not being a smart buyer. Can't you just hear in your mind a boss telling an employee to go buy an ink jet printer, ". . . but don't buy the highest priced model!"?

What else might s/he say? Probably, ". . . but don't buy the cheapest one, either."

Obviously you need to figure your costs for creating a new model. But you also need to look at how quickly those costs would be offset if the new model increases your percentage of sales for your higher priced Models #2 and #3, over your Model #1 (which undoubtedly has your lowest profit margin.

Now consider—how might this tactic work for your product(s)?

#20

Increase the "switching costs" for your buyers

If it will cost your buyers time and/or money to switch to a competitor of yours, you can comfortably raise prices to a premium position over your competition.

Example: Lotus 1-2-3, the first successful spreadsheet program, had a virtual monopoly for some time. After learning how to enter commands in their software, nobody wanted to learn another system.

Excel had a more advanced system which didn't require learning arcane codes and syntax. However, Excel would never have succeeded if they hadn't also made all of the Lotus 1-2-3 commands work on their program as well. Once they did that, users were willing to switch, because Excel lowered the switching cost.

Knowledge is the greatest switching cost for the Internet age

Look at www.LandsEnd.com. They have a custom department where you can enter your exact measurements and get clothing customized to your shape. It takes about 10-15 minutes to enter all your measurements and preferences. That doesn't guarantee that a customer won't go elsewhere, but it helps secure loyalty.

Why? Customers could enter their measurements at another site which offers this same custom service. But why take the time? LandsEnd gets customers to enter their data with Lands End first and, barring any unpleasant customer service problem, Lands End will have them for life.

How Amazon slipped up

Most people know how Amazon recommends new products to you, based upon your previous purchases. It probably earns them millions of dollars in impulse sales.

The biggest negative about this system is it doesn't distinguish between books a customer buys for him/her self and those bought as gifts. Example: I find their recommendations of little value to me, because they are loaded with books in which I have zero interest. Because they are topics I bought only as a gift.

A different idea could have allowed them to raise prices. Amazon allows readers to enter the names of their favorite authors in order to get a notification when a new book is released by one of those authors.

This is a great customer service, particularly for those readers who have a large group of authors they're trying to keep up with. It took about 20 minutes for me to track down copies of all my favorite authors, so I could add them all to Amazon's database. Believe me, I had no desire to do that ever again. Perfect for Amazon—a very high switching cost.

But . . . three problems cropped up:

1. Amazon.com often notified you of a "new" book that was just a re-release. The first couple of times I bought a book only to discover I'd already read it, I stopped trusting them and started to carefully look at each email.

2. They didn't make it easy to tell their database you already had a book, and there was NO way to tell it to assume you have ALL old books from your favorite authors and to notify you from now on only about *truly* new releases
3. After a time, their service stopped or became erratic. In some computer changeover, much of my list disappeared and I no longer could rely on their notification system.

Think, however, how big a value a truly customized database would be for someone who reads a lot. IF I could trust them to keep track of everything, then I would buy books only from them—because then their database would always be up to date. If I saw a cheaper price elsewhere, I'd probably not take it. That's because, to keep my Amazon database up to date I'd have to then manually enter the book I'd bought elsewhere. By buying only from Amazon, it would all happen automatically.

And, switch over to another book seller? No way. Even if they allowed me to do the same thing. The hassle would be far too great.

How can this work for you?

If you sell accounting services or medical services, you already take advantage of a somewhat-high switching-cost factor.

The real upside is for products or services that can be customized. The more you can take over an annoyance factor for your consumers, and make it go away, the more likely they are to stay with you, even at a premium price.

So the next think-tank session you have on improving customer service, consider this. Before thinking how much some new customization would cost—ask if it would raise the switching cost factor for your customers. If so, if you can provide real value in return for some work on your customers' part—look at that work as something that will help to keep them from switching to chase lower prices.

21

Upgrade your premises—store, website, kiosk

Why would upgrading your store or website allow you to raise prices without losing unit sales?

Here's a famous story to illustrate the point. It comes from a research paper titled Mental Accounting and Consumer Choice, by Richard H. Thaler:

Scenario #1:

You are lying on the beach on a hot day. All you have to drink is ice water. For the past hour, you have been thinking about how much you would enjoy a nice cold bottle of your favorite beer. A friend gets up to make a phone call and offers to bring back a bottle of your favorite beer from the only nearby place where beer is sold — a small, run-down grocery store. He says that the beer might be expensive and asks how much you are willing to spend. He says he will not buy the beer if it costs more than the price you state. What price do you tell your friend?

Scenario #2:

(Exactly the same as above, except "a fancy resort hotel" replaces "a small, run-down grocery store.")

As you might guess, the maximum amount consumers are willing to pay in the two above scenarios differs. Thaler found executives willing to pay $1.50 at the run-down grocery and $2.65 at the fancy hotel. The same study was repeated with Harvard MBAs and the differences in prices were similar. I've also conducted this survey, with undergrad and graduate business students. In all cases, students were willing to pay more at the fancy hotel.

Take a moment to notice how clever Thaler was. The normal reason given for paying more in a fancy hotel is the ambience. Right? Yet, Thaler has effectively removed ambience from the equation—after all, YOU're not going to benefit from any ambience. You're not moving from your beach towel.

In this scenario, why should you care where your friend buys the beer? Why would a buyer refuse to pay as much as s/he was REALLY willing to — if the beer came from a run-down grocery? The beer wouldn't be any less desired, or taste any less refreshing.

Isn't there some intrinsic "value" of a bottle of beer? Or of a cold bottle of beer when you're hot? Apparently not!

So, what does this mean for YOUR pricing?

It means that the "value" customers ascribe to a product is not a fixed number. And that value can vary dramatically depending upon the buyer's perception of your cost structure and image.

If you're a consultant, and you look hard-up or in need of the work — the perceived value of your services will be less than if you look like you're part of a larger firm... or if you look very successful... or if you seem very busy.

If you sell a product, and buyers can assume your cost structure is lower than that of other sellers — buyers will want a piece of that difference.

Thaler's study should just remind us that "value" is a moving target — and we, as marketers, can control at least some of its direction.

So, to be able to raise your prices, raise your "looks"!

HOWEVER . . . if your market position is the lowest-priced brand, make sure your "looks" are NOT classy. Those seeking only the cheapest will often turn away from a store or website that looks upscale—assuming they would have to pay more there.

#22

Offer upgrades as separate packages

This tactic is especially great when you have two very different groups of potential customers. For example:

1. One group who will find your product/service incredibly valuable and are therefore willing to pay top dollar
2. Another group for whom your product/service will be only somewhat valuable and/or which is very price sensitive

This works particularly well with training courses, memberships and software. Here's how Internet marketing guru Harmony Major once described it for her sales:

I always try to have different pricing levels for my products, which really can increase your response and conversion rate. Especially when your products/services are priced higher than normal.

We have to realize that there are people who'll need **each and every service** you include in that "premium" product, but that there are others who may not want to pay your premium price just to acquire or use a product or service that they'd only have use for **PART of.**

Because a lot of the times, it's not about whether or not your prospect has the money for what you're offering. It's about whether or not they feel that the price they're paying justifies *how many of the "pieces" of your product they'll actually* **use**.

Say, you're offering a product for $200 that includes phone consulting, a manual, and a 6-month website membership. Instead of making this the only package you offer, you can often **increase your profit and conversion** by offering several "pieces" of that same package separately, for a lower price:

PACKAGE #2 ($75):

- the manual

PACKAGE #1 ($150):

- phone consulting
- the manual

PACKAGE #3 ($200):

- phone consulting
- the manual
- the 6-month membership

The same is true if you begin with a product that's only $50.

I think people should introduce "premium" packages into their pricing strategy to take advantage of that extra income. Like offering a "Silver" or "Gold" upgrade offer that both cost more than the original $50 "Basic" offer.

This almost always increases profit, as you're able to break down the barriers of a lot more prospects (and even increase customer retention) by offering solutions that more closely match their needs.

—Harmony Major, 2004

This also works great with services

- Accountants could offer three different levels of bookkeeping for companies.
- Fast-food joints could offer three different sizes of their best-selling sandwich.
- Car repair companies offer different levels of "checkups" based upon the number of miles your car has driven.
- Spas offer half-day vs. full-day treatments, and could further specialize by the customers' goals. For example: *A Half-Day Tension-Relief* program could focus on massage, giving neck, back, foot & hand massages. *A Half-Day Beauty* program could focus more on facials, manicures, pedicures, etc.

Retail-sold products use it by establishing different models, running from basic to premium.

Clothing, however, would be a problem. You couldn't sell the same design in a sweater, with one version in alpaca and the other in nylon. Nobody would buy the more expensive version if it looked just like a cheaper version. You could, however, make some small but noticeable changes and then sell both versions.

#23

Add a small per-usage fee to your price

(But . . . only where you can easily see usage!)

This tactic can be very effective, but only a small group of products have thus far found it to work for them.

The value of this add-on fee is two-fold:

1. A small usage fee may be accepted as an add-on, thus raising your price, or
2. A usage fee may enable you to lower your "base" price substantially below a competitor—thus making your offering much more appealing—while still getting a price "increase" in your total revenues (base plus usage).

Who does this tactic work for?

- Syndicated newspaper columns
- Movies
- Phone companies
- Many B2B industries

There is one big caveat with this tactic. That is that you must be able to VERIFY the usage in a clear way that both you and the customers will agree upon. Let's look at some of the ways this is done:

User base

Where you cannot get a good read of actual usage, you can set usage fees based upon your client's customer base.

Example: Media have audited or agreed-upon subscriber/reader/viewer numbers. Newspapers are audited for their circulation by an independent audit bureau. So are magazines. Websites are ranked by the number of visitors per month. TV has its Nielson ratings. It is obvious that a newspaper with a circulation of 1 million can pay more for your syndicated column than one with a circulation of 10,000.

Syndicated columns charge a fixed fee plus a fee based upon your circulation. Content provided to websites could do the same—a fixed fee for all, plus increments based on the number of visitors.

Actual usage

Where a company can ascertain actual usage, this tactic is frequently used.

Example #1—cellphone service:

Phone companies have long based their prices on a flat base fee, plus a data-usage fee.

Example #2—copies:

Copiers were one of the biggest users of per-usage pricing—because for a long time you could only lease a copier, and the company which owned the machines could clearly see how many copies were made on each machine.

Percentage of revenues

Charging a percentage of the revenues your customers earn is a strong, easier-to-sell pricing strategy—but you again must be able to verify sales.

<u>Example #1—movies:</u>

Movie producers, distributors and theatres all share a percentage of the fees paid by movie goers, usually 50% to the theatre, 20% to the producer and 30% to the distributor. Despite the different nomenclature, this can also be viewed as a per-usage fee, as both the producer and the distributor get a "price" based partly upon sales.

<u>Example #2—media advertising:</u>

Magazines, newspapers, radio, and some cable TV shows which aren't selling very much advertising, are sometimes willing to run advertising space on a "P.I." (per inquiry) or revenue-share basis. Thus the advertiser pays the media a fixed fee per inquiry (in B2B, where the ad attempts to generate leads) or a fixed percentage of sales. What keeps this tactic from being used a lot is the trust issue— how can the media verify how many leads or sales the advertiser received?

How is this a "per-usage" pricing strategy? The media is setting up a separate price, available only when they have a "hole" or "remnant" space to fill (or where they can't sell enough ads the "normal" way) which they will price with no flat fee, but a per-sale, a per-inquiry, or a percentage of sales fee.

PART IV

PRODUCT REPOSITIONING THAT LETS YOU
RAISE PRICES

Sometimes you don't need to change your product—just how customers perceive it.

What is the "position" of your product? It's whatever customers THINK it is. Remember, for marketing ... perception is reality!

Here is how to change that perception so that customers will then perceive a greater value for your offering.

#24

Reposition your product into a higher-value category

One very successful tactic for getting a higher price is to reposition your product/service into a higher-priced group of products or services.

Note that this does not involve actually changing your product or service—just changing the perception and positioning of it.

This tactic is easier to understand by looking at examples.

Product example

You sell a face cream that keeps skin moist and helps hide wrinkles. Let's say prices of face creams are roughly $9 per jar. However, there are specialized treatments you can buy to hide wrinkles that sell for $39 for a small tube. You may be able to sell your jar of face cream for $15, by emphasizing how cheap it is comparing it to the $39 wrinkle-removal treatments.

Media example

You sell a newsletter on marketing for dentists. The price is $295/year. This seems like a high price to dentists, who are used to getting dental magazines for free. However, let's say a marketing consultant for dentists costs $1,500 per day. You may also know that the average amount paid to marketing consultants by dental practices is $15,000 a year. By repositioning your newsletter as an alternative to high-priced marketing consultants, a $295 price seems very cheap.

Service example

You sell accounting services to small businesses. Assume almost all of your customers buy just your basic service of doing the books monthly and preparing annual financial statements for tax purposes. Let's say there are 8-10 other people or companies in your town offering the same service and you all charge roughly $15,000 a year.

Could you reposition yourself as their outsourced Financial Comptroller—or VP/Finance—instead of their outsourced Accountant?

If so, your customers would expect to pay more. (Of course, you'd have to offer some additional services to make the difference believable.)

Now it may be that most of your customers won't buy any of those add-on services—because what they need is limited.

But . . . if your clients are offered an outside accountant for $15,000 a year, or an outside Financial VP for $15,975—and both would do the same services—which would they pick? Some will pick the 2nd option. Why?

- For piece of mind
- The for higher level of advice they would perceive they would receive

25

Reposition your product as leading to a higher-value end benefit

If your product or service becomes just a part of an overall end benefit to your customers, you may have opportunities for price increases.

For example, perfumes are sold not on their aroma, but on the end benefit of making the buyer irresistible to men. (Of course, great hair and fortunate genes are also an advantage!)

The "end-benefit effect" is an aspect of pricing strategy that recognizes two distinct phenomena:

1. The more price sensitive buyers are to the cost of the final product/service (i.e., the end benefit), the more price sensitive they will be for each of the components of that final product. For example, if someone is trying to build a back yard shed for the cheapest possible price, they will be very sensitive to the cost of the wood, roof tiles and other materials they use in its construction. However, if they're splurging on a hot tub, an extra $100 for a better top isn't likely to cause a blink.

2. In looking at the individual components of the final product, buyers will be more price sensitive to those components which make up a larger percentage of the total price. Using the shed example above, buyers will be more price sensitive about the cost of the wood than the cost of nails—because the wood might account for 80% of the total costs and the nails might account for 2%.

How to use this tactic to raise prices

1. Focus buyers on the high-value end product

Examples:

Let's say you have a lipstick that doesn't smear. And that lipsticks in general cost $6. How can you charge $7 or $8 for your non-smear lipstick? Take the focus away from your product and on to the end benefit—which is freedom from worry about looking bad. You could show someone who doesn't know her lipstick has smeared. And she's smiling at her boss—or a potential boyfriend. Maybe she's got the lipstick smeared on her teeth. Preventing such an embarrassment is worth more than $6 to women. Freedom from worrying about it is also worth more.

Internet publishers do this with "How to Make a Fortune on the Internet" e-books. They want to reposition their product away from being a "book." After all, bookstores have taught us all that books are not worth that much. Maybe $9? Maybe $19? But seldom more.

Instead, they position their e-books as inside advice from leading authorities. Their sales message is not so much about the 200 page product you'll receive, but the millions of dollars this product will help you earn. They're focusing not on the actual product, but on the end-benefit the buyer will receive from their product.

2. Emphasize your insignificance in the overall price

Normally we don't want to convince people of the insignificance of our products or services—and that isn't what we're saying here. The product or service should be perceived as a key part of the overall product/service—but an insignificant part of the price.

<u>Example:</u>

Party napkins are sold for prices substantially higher than the exact same napkins that are not positioned as good for parties. Why?

- Because they are brightly colored and "themed" (i.e., luau, fish, birthday). Because they are very visible.
- And—because their price is a small component of the overall price of the party.

If by spending an extra $10, you can make your party look more professional, more "fancy" or "better put together," then the extra $10 is a small addition to the total party cost to achieve this "end benefit."

But . . . it's not that the inherent value of napkins went up. This increased value is only due to the napkins' perceived effect on the party.

PART V

PACKAGING CHANGES THAT LET YOU RAISE PRICES

We're all suckers for a pretty—or handsome—face. Looks matter.

Sometimes all that's holding your product or service back from being able to command higher prices is the packaging in which it's wrapped.

Can you use one of the ideas in this section to make your product or service more desirable? More valued? Thus able to command higher prices?

26

Bundle your product/service with extras

This is one of the most-often-successful tactics for increasing prices.

Dede Hall, author of *The Starving Student's Cookbook,* had very poor sales for her books. Then one day she added an inexpensive skillet with the book and shrink-wrapped them. Then she took 150 of them to two stores that she thought wouldn't sell them. Yes, to her surprise, all 150 sold in two days. . . . She sold over 100,000 copies in a few months. Where? Price Clubs and K-marts.

Bundling your product/service with "premiums"

At its most basic, this tactic is nothing more than providing "premiums" as a reward for purchasing the main product. Magazines and paid-subscription newsletters have long used this tactic. Successfully.

However, much depends upon the desirability of the premium. When I headed magazines for Springhouse, we tested premiums for *Learning '99,* a magazine sold to teachers of K-8 grades. We tested a clear, inflatable world globe, a sturdy canvas briefcase, and a "teacher kit," similar to a zipper-closed tool kit, which included a ruler, stapler, scissors and other useful teacher tools. The inflatable globe didn't increase response enough to cover its costs. The kit was OK, but the briefcase allowed us to raise the price enough to more than cover its expense.

When I was a magazine publisher at CBS, I saw a fellow publisher take a money-losing magazine, *American Photographer,* and turn it into a winner by the use of bundling. He found a great-looking, sturdy black canvas camera bag, with plenty of inside pockets and cushioning, which he offered as a premium with a subscription. The bag looked like it should cost $25, but he was able to get them made in China for much less. Including mailing costs, the bag cost him $7 total.

By bundling the subscription with the bag, he was able to get a $10 higher price for the magazine, giving him (after paying for the bag) an extra $3 per order. With close to 200,000 subscribers, you can easily see what a profit windfall this was.

E-book publishers do the same, creating, finding or buying "bonuses" to give to buyers as added incentive to buy their e-books.

Bundling tactics beyond the "premium"

Premiums can be defined as something of less value than the "main" offer, although sometimes that line can be pretty thin. For example, while buyers of *American Photographer* undoubtedly liked the magazine, many of them may have really wanted that great camera bag!

This tactic can, however, be pushed far from the premium idea—to where your "main" product is an equal to its bundled partner—or is even inferior.

For example, I want to do a book on pricing new products. But ... as I got into it I realized that a piece of software could make it much more accessible to small business owners without a marketing background.

So I have been developing a software program. When it's ready, the software may end up more (or equally) attractive compared to the book—to some of my potential customers.

Here are some additional bundling ideas, to help get your creative juices flowing:

- Is your accounting service more valuable if it's packaged with a tax service as well?
- Could you bundle custom small bird cages, especially those for parakeets, with a separate "playground," including teeter-totter, bells, mirrors and more? Could you sell the combined package with a tag line such as: "For the luckiest bird in the world!" or call it a "Pampered Pet Deluxe Living Suite"?
- How about bundling dog life vests with "float-on-the-water" toys such as a frizbee, balls, and more?
- You've probably seen "snack packs" that include crackers, cheese and a few grapes. How about a "Low-Carb Survival Kit" that includes a snack acceptable for those on low-carb diets?
- If you're selling a new piece of technology, why not bundle it with some software or products/services that increase its value?
- If you sell manicures, why not bundle them with a neck massage or a facial for a 20-minute "spa" refresher?

The goal in bundling

As you consider possibilities, don't lose sight of the goal. The primary goal is to bundle with something that adds enough value in the mind of your customers, that you can INCREASE the NET CASH you make.

A secondary goal is to make your current product no longer directly comparable with competitor products, so potential buyers can't compare apples to apples and buy based only on price.

27

Break out parts of your offerings

If you already have a product or service that includes a number of components, there are two ways to get a price increase by unbundling them.

1. Itemize the component prices of your bundle, or
2. Actually UN-bundle your components

#1 Itemize the component prices of your bundle

Are your customers fully aware of all the value of the pieces of your offer? Often by itemizing the value of each component, you can raise the perceived value of the whole.

This tactic doesn't require you actually sell the components separately, just that you make sure a separate price tag is listed for each, adding up to a very large number—much larger than the price of the bundle.

Example:

Suppose you offer training programs for corporations. Your price sheet might include separate prices to establish the value of all your components, including:

- In-person training
- Training materials
- Followup training sessions
- Followup training materials
- Other?

The goal, of course, is to create a group of components that sound so valuable that you'll be able to raise the price of the whole with little to no resistance.

This works especially well when you can add components that have little cost to you but a high value for your customers.

Example:

Below is a breakout of a package a magazine could offer to a potential advertiser. The far right column (which would never be shown to customers) gives the costs of each component to the publisher.

Benefit	Price	[Incremental cost to magazine]
12 full page ads in XYZ magazine	$70,000.00	$0 (normal offer)
Right to mail magazine list once	$9,000.00	$300.00
Table at annual conference dinner	$5000.00	$2000.00
Editor to talk to your staff	$5000.00	$0.00
TOTAL	$89000.00	$2300.00

Note above that the add-ons to the ad pages have increased the value of your offering by $19,000, yet cost you just $2,300.

How you use this tactic is up to you. If your customers were seeking a price well below $70,000 for the ads, you may be able to use this to hold to the $70,000 price. Or you may be able to sell everything as a special package—maybe for $80,000.

An example of a special package is a "Wimbledon" package *World Tennis* magazine offered advertisers, which included ads in certain Wimbledon issues, hotel & meals in London, good tickets to Wimbledon, and attendance at special *World Tennis* events where they could meet with some of the players. It went for a hefty premium over added costs to the publisher.

#2 Actually un-bundle your offerings

There are fewer instances where this tactic works to allow you to increase prices, but if you fall into those instances, you may wish to try it.

Is one of your bundled components a "dog"?

You should consider unbundling two products or services IF:

- One of your bundled components has a low perceived value to customers,
- AND your competitors offer your main product without the "dog,"
- AND there is a cost to including the "dog" in the package

Given the above scenario, you would be able to save some cost from dropping the dog and either increasing your price for the main product (if viable given your competitive situation) or selling more of them if you don't increase the price.

However, if the "dog" component does NOT cost you money, you should probably not unbundle it. It may be what allows you to have a higher price than a competitor—or to at least differentiate yourself so potential buyers cannot compare apples to apples and buy only on price.

Are both of your bundled components big winners?

If you have two "winner" components, both highly desirable by customers, you may find that you can increase their individual prices by unbundling them. That would make each available to those who cannot afford both, or who already have one of the components.

In effect, you would be eliminating the discount expected by customers for buying two products together.

However, this should definitely be tested before unbundling them, as it could well decrease your volume of overall sales. The combo may be causing people who would not have bought one of the components (no matter that it is a desirable one) if it weren't with the one product they most desired.

28

Shrink your offering—without it being noticeable

One of the easiest ways to get a price increase is to shrink what you deliver. Instead of a 16 oz. bag of candy, you deliver a 15 oz. bag. For the same price.

As long as the weight of what is being delivered is clearly marked on the bag, there is nothing wrong with this technique.

If you sell single-serving yogurt, your customers may have a fixed price in their mind of what "lunch" or a "snack" is worth to them. Say your yogurt sells for $.99 for a single-serving cup (8 oz.). It might be hard or even impossible to raise your price to $1 or more for that cup; your volume losses could be too great. So you can get the same price increase by delivering a 7 oz. single-serving package.

Using this tactic when you do not sell food

Shrinking the packaging works well for any category of product that is packaged in multiples.

Hardware:

If you are selling bags or boxes of bolts or screws, you can reduce the number or weight of those packages and maintain your price—for an effective price increase.

Subscription products:

(Where you sell a year's worth of issues or website access for one price.)

It's more complicated in this field, because when a subscriber comes to renewal—you will lose some of them. So you need to know if you'll lose more than you gain by offering, say, a 9-month subscription.

However, it works very well for subscriptions if you are selling B2B, and your potential buyers have a dollar limit on the amount they can approve. Suppose you sell primarily to marketing managers. Research may show you that most of them have a limit of $300 in their approval authority; for anything over that amount they have to go to their boss to get approval. *(Note: in B2B, a price that requires approval from your customers' bosses will result in a big drop in sales.)*

Say your newsletter was priced at $299, but you really want or need a price increase. You could raise your price to $350 for a year, but make your primary offer—on your website and in direct mail—be $299 for 9 months.

Printed products:

Physical Size

You would be shocked at how much you can save by cutting a tiny bit from the size of printed products. For example, when I was a group business manager at CBS Magazines, I proposed to CBS that they cut 1/8 of an inch from the size of their magazines. It was a tiny shrinkage of the "packaging" of our magazines. Certainly not noticeable to buyers. But .. . it saved just my group of magazines over $250,000 a year. Each year.

Why? Some of the savings were in paper costs, but even more savings came from the post office. Reducing the weight by even this small an amount made a big difference because of the volume we were mailing.

The newsweekly magazines not only cut trim size, but they also cut the "weight" of the paper. After doing this several times, their pages became so thin they were practically see-through. Each cut of paper weight saved them a bundle. But . . . at some point you have to worry about the quality of what you're delivering because it becomes apparent.

Fortunately for the newsweeklies, thin paper doesn't matter to customers as much as it would on, say, *Southwest Art* magazine.

Units Delivered

Publications have found they can deliver fewer issues without losing a single sale. For example, I have cut monthly newsletters from 12 times a year back to 10 times — without anyone noticing or it affecting subscription sales at the same annual price.

Further, other newsletter publishers have seen the same customer indifference when they reduced a weekly from 52X per year to 48X. And a twice monthly from 24X to 22X. In all cases, it had no effect on customer demand for the newsletter at the same price as previously charged. But in all cases the net effect is a very healthy price increase for the publishers.

Services:

This reduction tactic can work on services if you can remove part of the service that was previously included and maintain your price. However, it is much harder to find parts of services that you can remove which are not noticeable to buyers. Reducing hand-holding, for example, would directly harm the perceived quality of your service.

The best and maybe only way to use this tactic for services is to find parts of the service that can be handled over the Internet. If you make it easier for your customers to send you orders or communicate with you electronically, you can probably find big savings in customer support.

UPS is a good example, as is FedEx. By creating excellent online systems for finding out where your package is at any point in time, UPS and FedEx have saved millions of dollars in support personnel who used to respond to customer phone calls for the very same package tracking. That, in effect, gives them a price increase because they have to spend less for each sale.

You don't have to be huge, however, to make this tactic work. If you require a chuck of information from customers, which previously they filled out on paper—you could have them do it electronically and save yourself re-keying the material.

29

Increase the quantity in your package

This tactic sounds counter-productive. How can INCREASING the quantity you deliver help you increase prices?

If the cost of your packaging is worth more than what's inside—this technique can work for you.

Example:

Let's say you produce a line of perfume. Your containers (bottles & packaging that holds the bottles) cost 75% of your total product costs, while the perfume itself makes up 25%.

What happens if you increase the size of what you're selling from 1 oz. to 1.5 oz.?

Consumers will see 50% MORE product. But . . . did your costs go up by 50%? Not even close!

Since the amount of perfume delivered has gone up 50%, you can assume the perfume part of your product costs went up 50%. But that was only 25% of your total costs. The cost of a bigger bottle and bigger packaging to hold the bottle will probably be just 5-10% more than the cost of a smaller bottle & packaging. After all, it's still just one bottle/container/unit.

If we assume the bottle & outside packaging went up by 10%, your total costs will have gone up 20% — to supply 50% more product.

Thus, the "value" to the consumer of what you offer has gone up 50%, but your costs have risen 20%. You can then put a price on the larger offering that is 35-40% higher and greatly increase your profit margins, while also delivering a high value and even a DISCOUNT(!) to your customers.

Truly a win-win scenario.

PART VI

DISTRIBUTION CHANGES THAT LET YOU RAISE PRICES

Yes, some price-raising opportunities are created by distribution changes.

Here are some for your consideration.

30

Sell direct—where you can

Can you sell direct—without alienating your distributors or retailers? If so, you can dramatically increase your "price" for those direct-sold items. By eliminating middlemen who take usually 50%, the same actual price will deliver a 50% raise to you.

If there is no problem, offer the product on your website, in addition to listing retailers where buyers may find your product.

HP.com used to be a good example of a company selling both direct and through retail stores. Today their site is all about selling direct — you have to go to the small print at the bottom to find dealers.

If you can't sell direct without losing distributors and/or retailers, there are still two ways you can get around the problem. Both, however, will require an investment on your part:

3 ways to sell direct—and minimize the blame

1. Form a separate online retail company

Retailers can be very sensitive to a manufacturer's website that takes orders instead of directing buyers to the retailers. You can keep your retailers happy by using your website ONLY to promote your product and list retailers where it can be bought.

Retailers are not as quick to hate retailer websites that sell your product. Odds are many of your retailers are already selling your product on the web. If you form a separate company, that operates as an online retailer, you may be able to sell your products for the same price as other retailers, but reap much higher profits on those sales.

Danger—you must treat your separate retailer the same as other retailers. No favorable terms, pricing, etc. Further, while you are not obliged to bring up this situation, neither should you lie if asked. And ... you will be most successful if your retailer company does not compete aggressively with your other retailers. That can mean holding back, not maximizing the money you COULD make from that company. The goal, remember, is to have your cake and eat it too —not to stuff your face at the risk of losing important retailers.

2. Create a new line of your product—that you will ONLY sell direct

You can also avoid competing with your retailers by creating a separate product—that looks different and has at least one different feature—that you do not offer to any retailers. It can be sold only by you, and again not from your main website. It should have its own website.

3. Give your retailers a specific period of time in which you won't compete with them

Spawn.com, since sold to McFarlane, had a great solution for selling action figures. They gave their retail stores a six-month exclusivity for each new action figure. During those six months, Spawn.com would not sell the figures on their website. After the six months, Spawn.com picked up a lot of profit by selling on their own website (where they didn't have to give the retail discount).

31

Sell different versions to different retailer types

To increase your revenue per item sold, it helps to differentiate your customers. Someone making $100,000 a year can afford to spend more on your product than someone making the minimum wage.

Unfortunately, if you sell through retailers, it's harder to get such a premium from those higher-income customers.

When I teach pricing to college marketing students, and present this problem to them, they often suggest charging Saks Fifth Avenue more than Sears. For the same product.

However . . . that's illegal. You can't give one retail chain a better deal than another retail chain—if they both buy the same quantity.

Example:

You produce a hair dryer. It costs you $5 and you sell it to all retailers for $9.50. The "suggested retail price" for it is $19.99.

Suppose your retailers include both CostCo and Macy's. And you know that Macy's is charging more for your dryer than CostCo—and thus getting a much fatter profit margin selling it.

You want your share of that extra profit.

How to get more profit from your upscale retailers

The easiest way to differentiate your product (and profits!) by retailer type is to create different versions of your product.

- One which appeals more to more upscale customers, and is more likely to sell to high-end retailers. And you can price it higher and price it to get a fatter profit margin.
- Another which appeals to price-sensitive customers, and is more likely to sell to lower-end retailers and carry a smaller profit margin for you.

One warning — you might need to have different brand names for the two products. Otherwise it will be harder to sell your upscale version into upscale stores.

32

Create a scarcity

A genuine scarcity is both difficult to create—and occasionally dangerous. But it can be incredibly profitable.

It's difficult because you have to first generate a real demand for your product. If it's scarce, but nobody knows or cares, then you can't profit from it.

It can be dangerous because a recognized scarcity will cause many potential competitors to investigate your market to see if they can't jump in and profit from the scarcity you created.

Easy scarcities to create—and profit from

If you can create a scarcity in something that others can never duplicate—you're home free. Consider the diamond industry. By controlling all the known diamond mines, this industry was able to set high prices (and profit margins). Because would-be competitors aren't capable of creating new genuine diamonds (only Mother Nature can do that), the scarcity has held. I'm told that there are enough diamonds in the mines that only this tightly regulated artificial scarcity has kept the value of a diamond from plunging to a tiny fraction of what they are currently worth.

The danger for the diamond industry is that high demand coupled with controlled higher prices has caused great creativity in potential competitors. In the diamond market, this has resulted in fake diamonds being created and sold that cannot be told from the originals until one has a jeweler's loupe or one tries to scratch glass with the artificial diamond.

Oil is another product where scarcity can quickly drive up prices. However, oil is considered essential for nations that have allowed themselves to grow dependent upon it. It's not a luxury, as are diamonds.

Thus, the danger for those controlling oil is that if they drive the prices up too high, they would create a strong incentive for other countries to attack them and take over their oil supplies. This creates an upper limit on how much profit oil owners can make.

The "fad" scarcity

Fad scarcities can be a wonderful thing for a manufacturer, except that they are almost impossible to predict. Hundreds of new toys, for example, are created each year and marketed with the hopes that they will become the "hot" new item. The one that kids across the country suddenly wake up and decide they MUST HAVE.

The "lucky" one or two toys that actually achieve this fad status cause their manufacturers to be swept onto a speeding roller coaster. You must create as many as you can—so you can sell while the fad lasts. But if you gear up to manufacture too many, you'll have wasted product when the fad suddenly dies.

Also, manufacturers can find themselves the owners of a scarce item —and also find that others, not themselves, are profiting from it.

A couple of years back, a car brand suddenly achieved scarcity. I think it was an Acura SUV. A friend of mine told me that the dealers couldn't get enough of them fast enough to supply demand. There was a waiting list. And the lucky few who could get one had to pay roughly $3,500 OVER the sticker price. But . . . the car manufacturer didn't pocket the extra money — this premium for scarcity ended up in the pockets of their dealers.

The artificial—or PERCEIVED—scarcity

It is much easier, and less dangerous, to create the appearance of a scarcity instead of the actual thing.

Such an appearance can often be created simply by adjusting marketing materials and offers. Here are some marketing lines that create the perception of scarcity, or at least the perception of scarcity at a lower price:

Phrases that imply the product is scarce—or difficult to find if you don't buy now

- Limit—[number] to a customer!
- Not sold in retail stores!
- Limited run! When these sell, the plates will be destroyed so no more can be created

Phrases that imply you won't be able to buy again at this low a price

- Prices going up [date]. Last chance to save!
- This low price is only guaranteed for today, [today's date]. *Note: there's a nice piece of javascript that will insert the current date in your website ad, changing it for each date at javascriptkit.com*
- Warning! This low price is only good for 15 minutes. After that, it will disappear and you will not be able to take advantage of it ever again. *Note, this is another great piece of*

code for website offers. It is sometimes accompanied by a clock or sand hourglass which shows the 15 minutes ticking (or dribbling) away. Once it's over, cookies on that person's computer assure they are no longer offered that discounted price. One example can be found here.

33

Stop gray market sales of your products

If you are selling at different prices in different countries, and those prices differ enough, you will find that profiteers are buying your product at wholesale in low-priced countries and reselling it at the going high price in other countries.

Thus, the profit from your high prices in country A are no longer going to you—but to a wholesaler in lower-priced country B, who is reselling your products in country A.

Manufacturers who have carefully priced their products to exactly meet the value of them in each country are often hesitant to then adjust those "perfect" prices. But . . . since you are no longer profiting from the increased margin in many sales to Country A, those higher margins are no longer a good reason for not changing prices.

Steps to protect your profits—and their limitations

If you can isolate those wholesalers who are doing the reshipping—you can put a cap on the number of products they can buy.

For example, pharmaceutical companies who have been making all their world-wide profits only from citizens of the USA are not happy about Canadian wholesalers who are reshipping sales to the US. They are trying to cap the quantities they are sending to wholesalers in the attempt to limit their "excess" product available to send to the USA.

However, as long as the price difference creates such a strong demand, ANY products they sell to Canada have the potential to end up in the US. If they limit quantities from some wholesalers, it would still be profitable for those wholesalers to buy up from other Canadian wholesalers—at a price higher than those wholesalers would get from selling to Canadian retailers.

The global market and especially the Internet as its distribution path, has made differentiating by country a much harder task. If there is a big enough demand or price difference, that differentiation may become next to impossible.

Another example: I was told about a book that was supposed to have good success in helping people stop smoking. I wanted to send it to a relative of mine. I checked amazon.com and it wasn't available for sale in the US. So I went to amazon.co.uk and found it—and bought it—there. This was a book specifically NOT for sale in the US. They were probably trying to negotiate a better distribution deal than they were being offered for US distribution. But I was able to easily circumvent this embargo.

So what can you do?

How much of your higher-margin profits is the gray market stealing from you? If it's a small percentage, it will probably best profit you to keep the price discrepancy between the identified two countries. If it's a large percentage, a financial analysis should be done to estimate the benefit of:

- Continuing the pricing status quo, or
- Reducing the price discrepancy between the countries by either raising the price in low-price countries or lowering it in high-price countries.

PART VII

PROMOTION CHANGES THAT LET YOU RAISE PRICES

These price-raising opportunities require you to change only your promotional materials and/or practices.

Some of these opportunities will affect your public relations campaigns, others are advertising-based, and one affects your customer-retention program(s).

34

Announce a forthcoming price increase

Sometimes companies with limited ability to test prices use the announcement as a test. They "announce" a coming price increase and watch for the reaction(s) of their customers. If they get only mild grumbling, they go ahead with the price increase.

If clients are calling them to say they'll be leaving when the increase goes through, the company can simply rescind the increase, or reduce the amount of the increase.

Using a price announcement to "talk" to your competitors

It is to your market's advantage to have "smart" competitors—that is competitors who avoid getting into a price war. Competitors who find other ways to compete than on price.

For example, if you have a competitor whose entire positioning is that they are the low-cost supplier in the marketplace, undercutting them is a bad move. It will always cause them to lower their prices further—to maintain their "lowest-cost" positioning. Then you're in a price war.

However, if all their competitors would RAISE their prices, the low-cost supplier in the market—unless s/he is a complete idiot—will also raise prices, while taking care to stay just under any other competitors.

The result? Everyone maintains their previous price positioning relative to the competition—but everyone gets 10% (or whatever the increase is) more on their bottom line. A win-win for all the sellers in the marketplace.

However . . .

It is illegal to discuss prices with your competitors—and certainly illegal for you and them to fix prices or agree to raise prices together.

What companies can do—with some caveats—is to announce a coming price increase and then see what their competitors do.

Thus if you (especially if you are a leader in your market) announce a price increase, you can wait and see if others in the market are smart enough to also announce an increase.

If they don't, you can rescind your price increase. For good reason—because your clients told you you'd lose business if you go through with it.

A month or two later, you might announce a price increase again—hoping this time your competitors have wised up. The previous time, they might not have gone along with you because they were hoping to steal business from you when you raised prices unilaterally. However, once they find you'll rescind your increase rather than lose business, they may reconsider—and announce an increase themselves.

Avoiding lawsuits

To make sure your price announcement is not taken as price fixing, talk to your attorney. These laws can change overnight and the ramifications are too steep to get it wrong. S/he will probably advise you to comply with the following two requirements:

1. Your announcement must be public. Private announcements are almost always presumed to be price fixing.
2. Your announcement must have a legitimate business reason. If signaling your competitors is the only purpose—it is illegal. An example of a legitimate business reason is announcing the coming price increase so your customers can factor that into their budget planning for the coming year.

Warning for Goliaths:

If you are the biggest player in your market, you need well-informed legal counsel on all aspects of your pricing. You are more at risk than smaller competitors for attracting the Justice Department's legal teams.

This is even more important if you sell in Europe. There are double standards in Europe regarding prices and announcing price increases. The leading company in any industry has more legal restrictions on their pricing actions than do smaller competitors.

35

Selectively market discounts to only your most price sensitive customer segments

While coupons and rebates allow your customers to sort themselves into price sensitive vs. insensitive groups, occasionally it's more helpful to make those determinations yourself.

Suppose your product or service is slipping—and you're contemplating an across-the-board price cut. (PLEASE don't do this without testing first. Often the price is NOT the problem!)

As an alternative to an across-the-board price cut—you could target promotions to only your most likely price-sensitive customers. Maybe target retired people. Or teens. Or blue collar families.

You can get direct mail lists of almost any group. Check out *SRDS Direct Response Lists & Data* at your local library.

My advice, if you're ready to buy, is to find a list broker who has clients in your industry. They can steer you away from lists that look good but are filled with names that don't buy your kind of product or service.

Selling online? You can create special—discounted—sales pages and place ads linking to those pages on sites that target your price-sensitive groups.

What if you find price is NOT the reason they're not buying?

If you do a targeted price-reduction promotion such as the above—and it doesn't increase response—you can be pretty sure that price was not the problem.

That leaves only a few dozen potential culprits for your declining sales, including:

- Customers have declined for ALL products/services in your category
- You don't seem as authoritative/credible/knowledgeable/capable as one or more competitors
- Your quality has declined—or the quality of your competitors has grown
- Your product/service features are not—or are no longer — as compelling as your competitors'.
- Your competitors' promotion materials are hitting bigger hot buttons than yours are.
- If you sell through distributors & retailers, your competitors could be offering them a better deal
- There could be bad word-of-mouth about you or your product—even if undeserved—on the Internet. Spend a few hours Googling yourself and your company.

• Hint: If someone has started a website titled **www. [yourcompany]sucks.com**, you have a problem!

• Another hint: Many companies buy up every URL they can think of that says something derogatory about their company. Examples: www.Boycott[YourCompany].com and www.hate[YourCompany].com. By doing so, they don't let one disgruntled person buy that URL and potentially damage their reputation.

#36

Announce how your costs have gone up

A surprisingly big part of how customers respond to price increases is their perception of how "fair" it is.

You can increase the chances that your price increase will be perceived as fair—if you can use one or both of the tactics below:

1. **"Our costs have gone up."** If your biggest costs have risen by, say, 5% and you're having a 6% price increase, it will almost always help customers to accept your increase if you inform them about this.
2. **"We can no longer avoid a price increase."** If you haven't raised prices in a year or more—it is smart to mention that fact when you finally do have an increase.

Sarah Maxwell (1995) researched what makes consumers believe prices are "fair." She found "a price based on cost" was by far the most cited. Thus price increases that are cost based are most likely to be acceptable. However, she also found customers saying a fair price was based on quality, market forces, value to the customer, "whatever is satisfactory to the buyer" and "a price based on negotiation." (Research reported in *Pricing Strategy & Practice*, 3(4), 21-27).

37

Get a celebrity endorsement

Raising prices when you get a celebrity endorsement is just common sense—how else can you pay the fat endorsement fee?!

Actually, paid celebrity endorsement doesn't seem to matter too much to already large companies—as far as providing price-increase opportunities. However, smaller ones with endorsements can sometimes increase prices. That's because without the endorsement they may be a no-name—lacking credibility. With the endorsement, they become a "player" and can therefore charge more than a company whose products/services are "unproven."

Most interesting, however, is what you can do if you get a FREE celebrity "endorsement."

Example of completely free endorsement

What does a small company do when Renee Russo tells *Good Housekeeping* that she uses their Frownies every night to ease wrinkles? This tiny little company, which had shrunk over the years to just a couple of employees—including the owner!—found itself facing HUGE demand almost overnight. Obviously, you put the pedal to the metal on manufacturing, and also obviously you use this opportunity to line up more and better distributors. But do you also increase the price? Doing so can help you in a "gear-up-quickly" mode, because it adds revenue you need and slows the demand a little. You do NOT want huge unfulfilled demand because it is like catnip to potential competitors.

When you can finally meet demand, then you can price test to see if your price can stay at the higher level, or if it would be more profitable at an even higher—or a lower—level.

Example of almost-free endorsements

If you have a striking product—something that catches the eye—you can provide it free to celebrities whose tastes/opinions carry a lot of weight with your target markets.

Then, if you get a photo in *Us* magazine showing the celeb wearing/using your item, it can mean increased demand.

That increased demand can be a good time to slip in a modest price increase—while your product is "hot."

#38

Get testimonials from REAL people/companies

Take a look at some of the biggest selling e-books and software on the Internet. (To see a wide selection, go to www.ClickBank.com. There are over 15,000 products offered there. Best of all, they are RANKED in order of how well they sell under each category.)

When you find the top ranked products in your field, you can click on the link and go directly to that product's sales page.

One thing you will find with the higher-priced products is lots and lots of real-person testimonials. Most of them provide links to the people/companies giving the testimonials. The best sales pieces even show photos of each person doing the recommending.

Downloadable e-books, video courses, and software run anywhere from $19 to $99—depending upon the authority figure, the topic, the strength of the copywriting, and the number of very believable testimonials they can attract. Yet often publishers use their great testimonials to increase their unit sales—without rethinking whether the price could also go up.

Direct response products/services are most likely to benefit from this price-increase tactic. That's because direct mail, websites, and infomercials give plenty of space to add plenty of testimonials. Products sold through print or broadcast ad buys, however, are less likely to be able to use this tactic to raise prices.

39

Stop giving discounts as customer retention rewards

So you have a group of loyal, devoted customers. People who would PREFER to buy from you instead of any of your competitors.

Why in the world would you then offer this group price discounts? The very group most likely to be willing to pay full price?

This is the height of foolishness posing as "customer retention rewards." Instead it devalues your price/quality/value to the very group that holds you highest in these qualities.

Of course you need to coddle these customers. Reward them. Pamper them. Even GIFT them. But that gift needn't be—in fact should NOT be—price discounts.

Consider Harley Davidson. Consider how strongly their customers identify with the company. Harley schedules events across the nation, where its customers can meet and bond with others like them and with the company. This is a great reward for your best customers. Much more effective than price discounts.

As a bad example, consider Starbucks. Their star rewards are given for every dollar you spend, and can be used for free drinks, food, anything. Most people who are very price sensitive are buying their coffees, etc. at McDonald's or Dunkin' Donuts. So why is Starbucks discounting prices that people are perfectly willing to pay?

If I were in charge of their loyalty program, I'd figure out something different with which to reward customers. Something bigger and impressive — that would take a lot of points to get but which would really mean something to their customers instead of just an occasional free drink. Right now, customers are cashing in their points occasionally for that free drink — but it doesn't really mean anything to customers not price sensitive. Starbucks is not getting much goodwill at all for the huge amount of money they're investing (losing!) with this program.

Good discounts

Not all discounts to your best customers are bad. For example, you can offer them discounts on additional or peripheral products. But NOT additional or peripheral products that almost anyone buying your base product is likely to buy.

Better "rewards"

Here are some ideas you may be able to adapt and use:

* Tickets to something

* Preferred seating to something

- *Example:* you get a jazz festival which is appearing in multiple cities to give you a block of preferred up-front seating. Your customers still buy a full-price ticket, but thanks to you they can get the best seating.

* Advance notice of things

- *Example:* Everyone wants to be in on what's "new." Alert your customers to what's coming & what's new in their category of interest. (E.g., you're Food Network and you alert your customers to travel plans of top chefs—and give chances for tickets to taping of their shows.)

* First chance to get something. Give your best customers a couple of weeks where only they can buy your new product. So they can impress their friends, or (in a B2B environment) get a head start on their competitors.

* "Thank you" gifts to everyone. These should be low-cost, but of real value to your customers. (Still cheaper than discounts! And they don't put downward pressure on your base price!)

- *Example:* I sent my newly published print book *The Tao of Pricing* to my consulting clients.

* "Thank you" gifts to only a few. You can buy a certain number of items and offer them to the "First 100 who email us" or the "First 50 who click on this link." This is likely to get your e-letters read much more quickly and carefully.

- *Example:* MarketingSherpa.com offered 5 or 10 copies of new marketing books free to the first people who click on a link. Book authors gave them the books because it is publicity to their target market.

The above list is hardly exhaustive of the kinds of rewards you could —and should—be offering instead of cash.

Think of ways to make your best customers feel appreciated and part of the "family." Most families don't give out $5 bills as gifts to each other. They are expected to think of something more personal, more considerate of the recipient's interests.

You KNOW your best customers' interests because you know what they're buying from you. Gift them accordingly. Something that shows you're thinking about them, personally.

PART VIII

SALESPERSON & NEGOTIATION CHANGES
THAT LET YOU RAISE PRICES

This section covers price increase opportunities in the following types of situations:

- Entering price bids
- Negotiating prices
- Helping salespeople garner higher prices

40

Make price concessions temporary

In price negotiations, the goal is obviously to maintain the highest price possible.

Sometimes companies find they must make a price concession for a number of reasons, including meeting a competitor bid, overcoming a problem, etc.

The problem with price concessions is that customers expect them to become the new status quo.

If you are giving a price concession for some specific reason, you should require a formal, written agreement that specifies this price is for one buy only.

Thus you can require on a purchase order that it list the "normal" price, that it list the reason for the discount, and that it state this discount is offered for this one buy only.

Preventing a price concession from becoming permanent is, in effect, a price increase for you.

41

Cut your product/service for price bargainers

If you sell in a negotiated-price environment, such as automobiles to consumers, or many B2B product/service sales, you will find this tactic of value.

The lead-in to a sale usually establishes what, specifically, the potential buyer wants in features or special services from you. You then present the price. Then, as a final tactic to get a lower price, the buyer claims s/he shouldn't have to pay that much because part of the product or service is of little or no use to him or her.

Examples:

> "Yes, your outsourced accounting services sound interesting, but we're already doing the cash caging, so that part of your service doesn't really add much. It's nice, but . . . If you could drop your price by $xx, it would better reflect the value of what you offer to us."

> "Well, I like the car, but you're forcing me with your 'standard' package to pay for power brakes, which I don't even like that

much. That's got to be adding at least $500 to the car price. Why can't we just remove that $500, so the car better reflects what it is worth to me—if your company wasn't trying to force those brakes on me?"

Using this tactic, you would say to each potential buyer that you'll agree to cut the price of that added, but not valued, feature—as long as you can remove it from what you deliver to them.

For the accounting services example, you'll have the customer do his/her own cash caging.

For the car buyer, you'll get them that car without the power brakes.

"Wait a minute!" you may be thinking. What if I really can't sell my product without some of the things in the "standard" package? For example, what if GM won't deliver it without power brakes?

This tactic can still be part of your price negotiation. Often the buyer is lying. They really do want this feature, but this excuse was the best "reason" they can come up with as to why you should cut your price below what you quoted them—or even below the price you two already negotiated.

Often when you tell them OK, that you'll write up the agreement without that feature, they'll be surprised that you can. With the car, they may even ask, "You can really deliver it without the power brakes —which are standard with this car?"

Upon hearing you can (heck, you could replace the brakes in your service department!), they may well reevaluate and say that after thinking some more, it might be more convenient (or more desirable) to go ahead with that part of the product/service still included.

Result? You just saved yourself however much they were trying to knock from the price. This is the hoped-for and best result.

What happens if they don't back down?

What if they tell you to go ahead and remove that feature/part from what they're buying?

It depends on:

If you CAN break out that feature

As long as you have previously agreed on the real "value" of that feature in the overall price, go ahead and deliver the product or service without it.

In the case of the cash caging, it may be a little more awkward for the company to do that aspect itself, but as long as you can adapt without it costing you more money, do so. It's part of pleasing a customer. And, there's every chance they'll quickly get fed up doing it themselves and then turn it all over to you for the previously stated extra fee.

If it would cost you to break out that feature

Using the car example, you could write it up and get their signature for the car without the power brakes. Then you take the order to the supervisor. If the supervisor refuses to change the brakes in the car, then it's up to the supervisor if they want to accept that price with the power brakes. If so, you at least know you have the sale at the highest price you were ever going to get for this customer.

Warning

Please note this technique is only good for a customer who doesn't really object to the feature they're trying to deduct. Who says something like, "Well, [feature] is nice, but I really don't need it." So you know their reaction to the feature is only based on money, not on actually disliking the feature.

This technique will backfire badly if you use it with someone who says up front, "I hate power brakes. I don't want them in my car."

42

Pay commissions on net, not gross

One of the quickest ways to raise your prices of items sold by salespeople is to pay their commissions based on the net, not on the gross.

Paying a commission on every revenue dollar brought in ignores the fact that some of those revenue dollars barely exceed costs.

Example:

Suppose you sell two versions of a B2B product:

1. Version A sells for around $900 and your company's costs are $700
2. Version B sells for around $900 and your company's costs are $500

Assume you pay 5% of sales as commission.

If your salespeople are paid a commission on revenues, they don't care which version they are selling. They just want to make the sale—even though there's a big difference to your company which is sold.

Example:

Suppose you sell a product that costs you $6,500, and your salespeople are paid 5% of what they sell. Suppose they can negotiate price anywhere from $9,000 down to $7,500.

How likely are they to fight hard for a sale closer to $9,000 than to $7,500?

You might think they would fight hard—because they're losing 5% of any reduction in price. However, it is much easier to sell MORE products to more people—at $7,500 than to fight hard with each customer to increase what they pay. Salespeople are more likely to go for volume than for profit margin.

What can you do?

Here are a number of sales compensation plans that would encourage your salespeople to, in effect, raise the prices you are getting:

- Pay a fixed percentage on revenues, but pay a bonus percentage on everything they sell over an agreed-upon base. Thus in the example directly above, they might get 4% of all sales, but an extra 6% of all sales of this specific product over $7,500 per customer.
- Establish a base, which is the price salespeople cannot go below. Pay them x% for sales at that price; then x+% for sales from that base up to 10% above it; then pay x++% for sales from 10% over to 20% over, etc. etc.
- Reward sales of high margin products at a different rate than sales of lower-margin products. (Watch out, however, that the difference isn't enough to cause your salespeople to try to force their customers into a less-than-optimal-for-them buy. Buyers are very aware when sellers try to lead them to something not as good for their circumstances—and they

assume the salesperson is caring more about their commissions than about their customers.)

#43

Reposition your price

Use the "end-benefit effect" tactic in pricing strategy to reposition how your customer thinks about your price.

This works best in B2B sales, and if your product or service meets BOTH of these two criteria:

1. Your product/service is a small part of your customers' overall expenses, AND
2. Your product/service is critical to your customers

Let's look at each of these separately.

#1–Your product/service price is a small part of your customers' expenses

This tactic won't work if your product or service is a major part of your buyers' expenses. For example, if you supply lumber to builders.

Examples:

- You supply a training program for Company XYZ's consultants. This program teaches those consultants to use a piece of software that helps them service THEIR customers. Company XYZ's most expensive costs are salaries for those consultants, not your training program.
- Your company supplies buckles to a roller-blade manufacturer. The manufacturer's biggest expense by far is marketing, not the cost of your buckles system.

#2—Your product/service is critical to what your customers sell

Note that in each of the two examples above, your product or service is critical to the quality of what your customers sell.

If a consulting company doesn't have well-trained consultants, they won't be able to keep their clients.

Substandard buckles are easily noticed by roller blade buyers, and could damage the reputation of a manufacturer whose skate buckles break.

How IBM has used this tactic

IBM mainframe computers have always been priced higher than alternatives. But IBM recognized that computers cost far less than many other company expenses, such as personnel, marketing, manufacturing, etc.

IBM also recognizes that if a company's computers go down, even for a day, the cost to a company can be catastrophic. Certainly for those selling on the Internet, it could mean thousands of dollars for every HOUR the computers are down.

Thus IBM has always sold security—more than it sold computers.

This security is two pronged:

1. There is the perception that the computers are less likely to break down if they're IBMs, than if they're a cut-rate brand.

2. If they DO go down, IBM has the fastest response time of anyone. They smother you with service, including replacement computers if needed for an interim—and the personnel to make it happen faster.

IBM has bragged that if a company's computers ever go down, the response IBM delivers will make that company a customer for life.

How can this work for you?

At price negotiations, you can expect to be hammered about price. Your job is to keep the customer's eye on the ball, which is:

- The price of your product or service is a small one in their overall cost structure.
- Your product or service is also critical. If there are problems with it, it will cost your customer big money — either in fix-it expenses or in lost customers.
- It's not smart to risk big problems in a critical component just to save a few dollars. This is not the place for bringing in a cut-rate alternative.

44

Train your salespeople to uncover price INsensitivities

Salespeople need specific training in how to recognize opportunities for increased prices. And they probably need specific rewards based on this—in order for them to actually pay attention, instead of just trying to close the sale.

A customer in each of the following scenarios will be recognized immediately by a good salesperson as a "hot" prospect. What they ALSO need to do is to step back and think about just how "hot" the prospect is—and what that means for the price that should be quoted.

Where time is rushed

If your prospect is on a very tight deadline, or needs what you sell inordinately fast, this is an opportunity for increasing your price.

"Rush job" charges are common in many industries. They are important for companies that have a posted price schedule—so all can see. In that case, tacking on a rush charge is only fair, and usually expected.

However, if you don't post your "normal" prices, there is no need to itemize a surcharge for rush service in the bid you submit or the price you quote. Just quote for delivery on xx day, which highlights the rush aspect of the job. And do increase your bid to more than cover for the extra attention such a rush order requires.

Where there's a high cost to price shopping

If an out-of-town company is seeking your services, delivered in your local area, this is also a golden opportunity for increased prices. Particularly if you come recommended by someone in the prospect's home city.

Examples:

A. You handle employee law in Los Angeles, and a New York company contacts you regarding handling a lawsuit by a California employee. Your firm was recommended to the company by its New York law firm, which has heard of your good reputation in this field.

B. You're a home builder, based in Hilton Head. A satisfied customer of yours recommends you to a New York based CEO who is planning to build a vacation house in Hilton Head.

Why are these good opportunities for premium pricing? Because the cost to the prospect of researching alternatives in the area is very high. They don't know the local market. And they know there can be a big difference between a company that looks good on paper and one that actually is good. You come recommended by someone they know. Maybe even someone they trust.

Such a prospect is unlikely to launch a full-scale investigation into alternatives if you quote a price that is 5-15% higher than you would have quoted to someone not in this specific situation.

And . . . even if they do notice a price premium of this size, it's unlikely to kill the deal.

Where the "end benefit" effect works in your favor

A prospect that is gearing up for a big expansion—or one running at full capacity—is trying to keep his/her eye on the big picture.

That means you have an opportunity for premium pricing—IF your product or service is a small cog in their big wheel.

The purchasing director is going to be watched closely as to the kind of price or discount they get for the most important, most expensive products/services needed in their operation. They will likely not get a single kudo for saving a few cents on your product. In fact, they could even be criticized for spending time and attention on such a small item, when they should be prioritizing on what really matters.

If you can provide what is needed, on time, with no hassle, this has more value to such a prospect than saving an extra 5-15%.

If they are sure you can deliver acceptable quality, on time, with no oversight needed, then it is to their benefit to give you a quick yes, and check that item off their list. So they can move on to more financially critical parts of their desired end result.

45

Make it harder for customers to negotiate price

Protect your salespeople

One of the first questions many customers ask a salesperson is if they have the authority to negotiate price. If the answer is yes, your salesperson can look forward to being beaten up badly on price.

Consider making the answer a "no."

Some companies pair this policy with one requiring a signed purchase order at the desired price before a salesperson can go to management requesting a price break.

Protect your prices from your CEO(!)

I saw a study, although I can't remember the source, that showed the companies with the lowest profit margins on negotiated prices were those where the CEO of the company handled a lot of sales.

Apparently, it is very difficult when you run the company to tell a key customer that you won't be cutting him/her a deal.

If you're the CEO of your company, or if your CEO must have a strong sales function, consider creating a pricing department which must approve any price variations. All requests for price changes must be approved by them. A CEO has a couple of ways to transfer the "blame" to this department. Here are possible tactics to modify and try:

- "I can't undercut my pricing expert [name]. I need him/her to keep this company running smoothly."
- "I stay out of any pricing decisions. I let my pricing department handle all pricing so I don't have to listen to them explain it to me!"

However, as you can see from the above, holding the line on price is much easier if your customers are talking to a sales person instead of the CEO.

PART IX

PRICE-RAISING OPPORTUNITIES PROVIDED BY YOUR COMPETITORS

This last section looks at opportunities your competitors provide for you to raise your prices.

Every time a competitor raises or lowers their prices, they are giving you an opportunity to increase your profits. (Or, if you're not careful, an opportunity to lose profits!)

With Tactic #47 and with the downloadable 1-2-3 Price Change Model^{TM} (instructions under #47), you will now be better able to judge the consequences of changing your prices along with your competitors—or going in your own direction.

#46

When competitors raise their prices

One of the easiest ways to raise prices without paying a penalty in sales volume is when your competitors raise theirs. Very simple, right?

Well ... yes and no.

Unfortunately, many companies do not capitalize on this opportunity, for a number of reasons:

A. They don't find out about it

B. They don't raise their prices, because they hope to gain sales on their competitor

C. They don't know how to evaluate it

Let's look at each of these problems:

A. How to find out if your competitors have raised their prices

Some companies see their competitor prices clearly, and don't have to wonder if they have been raised. Others are not as fortunate. Here are some tactics for keeping up to date on your competitors' prices.

Retail pricing (online & off)

If you compete with one or more retail stores in your town, or with a number of national websites, you need to price shop. Look at your sales for the past 6 months—and (if your sales are very seasonal) look at them for the same month the previous year.

- What are the top 10-15 items that make up most of your UNIT SALES? (Sometimes people come to your store/website for a lower price on a frequently-bought item, but stick around to buy more. Your prices on those items that are price-shopped are important in bringing people into your store.)
- What are the top 10-15 items that make up most of your PROFITS? (Sometimes you make more profits from your normal 15 sales/month of a high-profit-margin product than from your normal 100+ sales of a low-profit-margin product.)

Once you've found the key products that are most important for your store/website (both those that bring in people and those that generate the greatest profits for you), you know what prices are important to your financial health. You need to keep current on what your competitors are charging for those specific products.

Websites:

If your competitors are websites, you simply have someone price shop your competitors for specific products at specific times and keep records of them. Once a month might be good in a market with few changes, but you may find dramatic price changes in any of these situations:

- The month before a holiday
- Holiday eves
- Weekdays vs. weekends
- 9-5 (roughly) vs. evening hours
- In-season vs. off-season

Physical stores, large cities:

In a large city, you can simply have an employee walk into your competitors' stores and look at their prices for your selected items.

Physical stores, small towns:

If you have a single competitor in a small town, and they know you and all your employees, what can you do? You can try to hire someone just for this, a baby sitter, or someone else whose connection to you might not be known. Instead, I'd go into the competitor's store myself, with a notebook. I'd be friendly and say I like to periodically drop in and check out other stores. I'd also say, "Feel free to drop in and check out my store in return."

Be very careful what you say to a competitor because you don't want to be sued by consumers for price collusion. It would be best if you go in when there are lots of people in the store, so everyone can see you didn't have a price conversation.

The first time you do it, you should hope to see a return visit from your competitor. You want them to see that you aren't pricing their products in order to undercut them. (But you cannot say this to them!) You want them to see your products are priced the same, or even slightly higher.

Consulting or other professional services

Lawyers & accountants:

These prices depend upon many things, including your town, your specialty, your credentials, and your office décor. [Don't laugh, there are a number of studies showing people expect to spend more when they go to a place with fancy décor (or a high-rent address) than when they go to lower-rent-looking facilities.]

Given that, the best way to discover what your competitors are charging is to ask their clients and/or ask others in your field who are not direct competitors. For attorneys, there may also be court records showing attorney expenses, usually giving an hourly rate.

Just know that there is a movement afoot to bill attorney and accounting services by the job, not by the hour. If you are a member of either of these professions, especially accounting, I recommend a great book, *Professional's Guide to Value Pricing*, by Ronald Baker. While the author gets up on a soapbox in this book, there are still some very useful forms and examples. At the least, it will give you a lot to think about.

Freelance services:

Uncovering competitor prices for freelance work can be done using the method(s) described above for attorneys and accountants, or you can use the methods below for consulting. Also, there are websites where people list their freelance skills and projects they can do—and frequently their prices. Examples: www.guru.com, www.upwork.com, www.fiverr.com, www.contractedwork.com, and many more. (Do a Google search for "freelance work" and "contract work" and you'll find many more.)

Further, there is likely to be an association you can join for your field, for example one for travel writers! Again, you have to be careful that nothing you say or do can be construed as trying to fix prices. But you are certainly allowed to poll other companies/freelancers to see what the going rates are.

Sometimes associations or consultants do pricing studies which you can buy.

Consulting services:

Uncovering "going rates" for consulting is very difficult. That's because almost every job is truly unique. In this instance, it is critical for you to get to know other consultants in your field. Attend conferences or places where you can network. Find out if a friend knows one of your competitors. Use that as leverage to call other consultants and ask them about pricing. Just be sure you ask more than one consultant. One might lie. Two or more will give you better protection.

There's an excellent book specifically on pricing for freelancers / consultants, called *What to Charge: Pricing Strategies for Freelancers and Consultants* by Laurie Lewis. In it she gives alternatives to asking a blunt and potentially legally dangerous, "What are you charging?" question to competitors. Here are two examples:

"A client has asked me to do [type of work]. Do you know anyone who's done this sort of job who might be willing to talk to me, especially about rates?"

"A client approached me about doing [type of work]. Do you have any pricing suggestions for me?"

B. What's wrong with letting a price-raising competitor twist in the wind?

You may think that a competitor raising prices is wonderful— because you can leave your price where it is and steal some of their customers. What's wrong with this? Because, if you actually do steal some customers, your competitor is likely to lower their prices again. Then you're back to square one. Your new customers are likely to return to your competitor. After all, when you were priced the same, they picked your competitor, not you.

Let's look at an alternative. Suppose when your competitor raised prices, you raised yours an equal amount. Now what will happen? If the two of you are the only real competitors in the marketplace, it is likely you will both keep the customers you already have. No change. But . . . you will each be making a much fatter profit, because you will be getting in more money for the same amount of work.

You should also know that unilaterally raising prices is something that smart companies often try to do, in order to "signal" to the marketplace that everyone should raise their price. They do that instead of calling up all their competitors and suggesting everyone raise their prices—because the latter tactic is illegal!

Sometimes this is done as an announcement that Company A is going to raise their rates effective [date]. If their competitors don't come out and announce they too are raising their rates, then Company A will not go ahead with the increase.

What does all this mean? If your #1 competitor announces a price increase or goes ahead with one, you should consider following.

C. How can you evaluate whether or not you should raise prices?

While there is a lot to say for raising your prices when a competitor does, sometimes it does make more sense to not join them.

How can you tell?

Typically the fatter your profit margin, the more you need to consider not raising your prices. If your profit margin is under 15% — you will probably be better off raising your prices when a competitor does.

But... run a break-even analysis (see tactic #47 following) to be sure.

#47

When a break-even analysis tells you it's smart to raise your prices

A break-even analysis is a simple calculation that packs a lot of wallop. It can help you make easy decisions to raise your prices—or not. It can tell you what to do when a competitor raises prices—or lowers them.

It can also surprise you. Seat-of-the-pants logic can often be proven completely wrong.

To do the analysis, you need only enter three numbers:

- Your current price
- Your current costs for one product/service you sell
- Your competitor's price increase (as a percent)

Two spreadsheets (two tabs on a single Excel^R file) make up the 1-2-3 PriceChangeModel^{TM}. It is available to you as a purchaser of this book. You can find it at: PricingPsychologyInstitute.com/ pricechangemodel. The password is HelpBizPrices.

When your competitors raise their prices

Running one of the spreadsheets will tell you what to do if your competitors raise their prices. For example, suppose you are considering leaving your prices as they are, in the hopes of stealing business from your now-higher-priced competitor. The analysis will tell you exactly how much your sales will have to increase to make that decision correct.

Should you leave your prices where they are? Suppose the analysis says you'd have to increase sales by 25%. If you think there's no chance of that happening, then the analysis has told you you'll be better off raising your prices along with your competitor.

Suppose the analysis tells you that the break-even number is 4%. You may be very confident that your sales would go up by a lot more than 4%, and thus your decision is again easy—don't raise your prices.

Unfortunately, sometimes the number given in these results is not so clear cut. You may find yourself saying, "I'm not sure. Maybe my sales would go up by this percentage. But I don't know." Sometimes you can examine your uncertainty and decide which way is more likely. If you're completely on the fence—I recommend you increase your prices. If you and your competitor raise prices, it is more likely others in your industry will also raise prices, which can lead to a much healthier profit margin for all.

When your competitors lower their prices

This same spreadsheet will help you calculate what you should do if your competitors lower their prices. Many companies have a knee-jerk reaction to this, and automatically lower their prices as well.

Your spreadsheet will just as easily let you look at the results of NOT lowering your price. You may find you'll make far more profits by not meeting their price. And... avoiding price decreases is really on a par with raising your prices: They can both lead to more money in your pocket.

When you are considering unilateral price changes

Finally, the second worksheet (tab) of the 1-2-3 PriceChangeModel™ will help you calculate what will happen if you unilaterally raise your prices—or lower them.

I strongly recommend you run this part of the spreadsheet as soon as possible.

Here we look at whether YOU should initiate a price increase—even though your competitors have not.

You should run this analysis whenever prices or costs in your market change. That might be every six months for some businesses—and every 6 weeks for others. It's fast and easy — you need to include only three numbers in the model to get your answer.

Reading the results of unilateral price changes

Sometimes the results of the break-even analysis are crystal clear.

Examples:

- **Yes—Raise them!**

• You may be considering a 5% price increase. You run the analysis and see that you will come out ahead with your 5% price increase as long as you don't lose more than 18% of your units sold. You may be very sure that a 5% price increase will NOT decrease demand by that much. In this case, you see an opportunity to raise prices.

- **No—do NOT raise them!**

• Alternatively, you may see that the 5% price increase you're considering will only be positive if your units sold drop by less than 2%. You may believe there is a very good chance of losing more than 2% of your unit sales. In this case, you know not to raise prices.

- **Your path is unsure!**

• If you're unlucky, you will get a result where you won't know the answer. It might say that you should raise your prices by 5% only if sales will not drop by 6%. You may have no idea if sales will drop 6%.

• If this is the answer you get, then you will need to utilize some of the other tactics in this book in order to successfully raise your prices —and your profits.

AFTERWORD

So, what's next for your business? How are you going to use this book to make your business stronger and to grow your wealth?

Have you already tried some of these tactics? Or did you read the book before doing anything?

In some ways, this book is like a diet book. Reading a diet book won't make you lose weight (darn it!) – you have to then ACT upon what you read. The same here. Reading this book is nice, but it won't put a cent into your pocket until you start using some of these tactics.

Unsure where to start? Let me suggest these three:

- #12, testing higher prices
- #2, moving your prices up to the next barrier
- #47, running the computer break-even analysis

If you regularly test parts of your offer (packages, headlines, other), the next time I recommend you test two higher prices—one you think you might get and one higher than that.

Sometimes the limitations on our wealth are only those we put there ourselves. For example, for a $295/year newsletter, I once tested both

$395 and $495. Thank goodness I tested the highest price because $395 was a dog, while $495 was the winner!

So to this day the publisher is banking an extra $200/year profit from each subscriber.

ABOUT THE AUTHOR

Marlene Jensen is the author of three additional books on pricing strategy:

- *Pricing Psychology Report*
- *Setting Profitable Prices*
- *The Tao of Pricing*

Today she offers online pricing courses at PricingPsychology.com and publishes a pricing blog at PricingPsychologyInstitute.com.

Dr. Jensen taught pricing at the university level for Lock Haven University (13 years) and for Western Connecticut State University.

Her doctoral dissertation was on pricing new products.

As a researcher, she conducted 32 studies on different aspects of pricing strategy.

Dr. Jensen worked in industry for 30 years, including marketing stints at ABC and CBS. Subsequently, she was president of Pricing Strategy Associates, which consulted on pricing for a number of large and small companies.

CONTINUE YOUR PRICING JOURNEY!

If you want to:

- Know the **2 biggest pricing mistakes** made my most companies, check out the free video at www.PricingPsychology.com
- Get a **free weekly pricing tip** to keep you thinking on the topic, subscribe to the Pricing Tip of the Week. The signup is at PricingPsychologyInstitute.com — just scroll down to find it.
- **Analyze a few of your most important prices** — so you get the most possible profits from each — check out the Pick Your Price video course at www.PricingPsychology.com.
- See what **other books on pricing** are available to you, go to https://pricingpsychologyinstitute.com/pricing-books/